"十二五"普通高等教育本科国家级规划教材

新闻英语视听说

BROADCAST NEWS ENGLISH （第五版）

主编 王 哲
编者 王桃花 陈 慈 谢 芳 齐金鑫 肖明文
　　　郭 曼 李继红 徐 辉 杨正刚 周文萱
　　　胡婧菁 许 伊 黄宇芝

清华大学出版社
北京

内 容 简 介

本教材的素材取自近年来国内主流英语媒体和欧美澳等主要英语国家的电视媒体公开播送的新闻内容，旨在帮助学生熟悉并掌握新闻英语的特点，进一步提升英语语言技能，包括听懂英语广播电视节目、及时获取现代资讯并灵活自如地用英语进行国际沟通的能力。教材内容具有视听结合、题材广泛、语言规范、兼具实用性与趣味性的特点。教材还配有原声剪辑视频，视频以现代美式英语为主，同时涉及不同的英语变体。教材涵盖前沿资讯、国际交流、风俗习惯、文化背景等方面的知识，以满足各种英语视听任务和口语交际活动的需求，从而真正提升学生的新闻英语视听技能和口语表达能力。教材另配有电子课件，读者可从 www.tsinghuaelt.com 下载使用。

本教材适用于英语水平较高的本科生、研究生及其他英语学习者。

版权所有，侵权必究。举报：010-62782989，beiqinquan@tup.tsinghua.edu.cn。

图书在版编目（CIP）数据

新闻英语视听说 / 王哲主编 . -- 5 版 . -- 北京：清华大学出版社，2025.3. -- ISBN 978-7-302-68253-0

Ⅰ. G210

中国国家版本馆 CIP 数据核字第 2025EX2830 号

责任编辑：刘　艳
封面设计：子　一
责任校对：王荣静
责任印制：刘海龙

出版发行：清华大学出版社
网　　址：https://www.tup.com.cn, https://www.wqxuetang.com
地　　址：北京清华大学学研大厦 A 座
邮　　编：100084
社 总 机：010-83470000
邮　　购：010-62786544
投稿与读者服务：010-62776969, c-service@tup.tsinghua.edu.cn
质量反馈：010-62772015, zhiliang@tup.tsinghua.edu.cn

印 装 者：涿州汇美亿浓印刷有限公司
经　　销：全国新华书店
开　　本：185mm×260mm　　　印　张：13.5　　　字　数：307 千字
版　　次：2004 年 10 月第 1 版　2025 年 3 月第 5 版　　印　次：2025 年 3 月第 1 次印刷
定　　价：58.00 元

产品编号：109906-01

前言

《新闻英语视听说（第五版）》是一本依据党的二十大报告精神和《大学英语教学指南》（2020版）编写的高级新闻英语视听说教材，适用于英语水平较高的本科生、研究生及其他英语学习者。

党的二十大报告指出，要"讲好中国故事、传播好中国声音，展现可信、可爱、可敬的中国形象。加强国际传播能力建设，全面提升国际传播效能，形成同我国综合国力和国际地位相匹配的国际话语权"。本教材旨在培养学生熟练运用英语的能力，能够"会讲、讲懂、讲好中国故事"，并帮助他们拓展全球视野、掌握国际规则、精通国际谈判。通过本教材的学习，学生能深入接触国内外优秀文化，获取新闻信息，增强跨文化交际意识，提升国际沟通能力，从而全面提高国际传播效能。

本教材的素材取自近年来国内主流英语媒体和欧美澳等主要英语国家的电视媒体公开播送的新闻内容，旨在帮助学生熟悉并掌握新闻英语的特点，进一步提升英语语言技能，包括听懂英语广播电视节目、及时获取现代资讯并灵活自如地用英语进行国际沟通的能力。教材内容具有视听结合、题材广泛、语言规范、兼具实用性与趣味性的特点。教材还配有原声剪辑视频，视频以现代美式英语为主，同时涉及不同的英语变体。教材涵盖前沿资讯、国际交流、风俗习惯、文化背景等方面的知识，以满足各种英语视听任务和口语交际活动的需求，从而真正提升学生的新闻英语视听技能和口语表达能力。

《新闻英语视听说（第五版）》共12个单元，涉及教育、人物、食物、旅游、时尚、生活方式、运动、娱乐、商业、技术、文学和自然等领域；形式多样，内容丰富，基本能够满足各种情境下的新闻英语需求。所有视听材料均配有文本，练习题附有参考答案，以辅助学生进行自主学习，并帮助教师进行课堂任务检查。本教材在语言、内容和语体等方面由浅入深、循序渐进，教师和学生可根据实际情况灵活调整，有针对性地使用本教材。

本教材强调新闻的时效性和使用过程中的互动性，学生可以通过扫描书中的二维码获取相应的视频资源。

由于编者水平有限，且编写时间紧迫，书中难免存在疏漏和错误，恳请广大同仁及英语学习者批评指正。

编　者
2025年3月于广州

Contents

Unit 1   **Education** ·· 1
       Part A   ChatGPT in the Classroom ········· 2
       Part B   Future of Education: How Is AI Affecting the Study of the Humanities in China? ·· 5
       Part C   No Smartphones on Campus ····· 7
       Part D   Tuition-Free ································ 9
       Part E   Projects ······································ 10

Unit 2   **People** ·· 13
       Part A   Martin Luther King's Legacy ····· 14
       Part B   Henry Kissinger Died at 100 ··· 18
       Part C   Queen Elizabeth II Died at 96 ··· 20
       Part D   Zhang Guimei, a Dedicated People's Teacher ·· 23
       Part E   Projects ······································ 24

Unit 3   **Food** ·· 25
       Part A   The Ultimate Chinese Food Tour—Peking Duck in Beijing ············ 26
       Part B   Study Finds Highly Processed Foods Linked to Early Death ············· 29
       Part C   Seawater Rice—A Solution for Global Food Security ······························ 31
       Part D   Future Food—The Menu of 2030 ··· 33
       Part E   Projects ······································ 35

Unit 4   **Travel** ··· 37
       Part A   Spain's Tourist Hotspots Facing Housing Crisis ··························· 38
       Part B   How "Trashy" Tourism Threatens World-Famous Destinations ····· 41

	Part C	Rise of Adventure Tourism ······ 43
	Part D	What Happens When You Use Your Mobile Phone in the Largest Resort in the World? ·················· 44
	Part E	Projects ································ 46
Unit 5	**Fashion** ·· **47**	
	Part A	Is Virtual Shopping the Future? ··· 48
	Part B	Style Meets Tech at Guangdong Fashion ·························· 50
	Part C	Why Milan Leads the Fashion Pack? ···························· 53
	Part D	Becoming Her Chinese Women's Fashion Evolution in the Past 70 Years ···························· 55
	Part E	Projects ································ 56
Unit 6	**Lifestyle** ·· **57**	
	Part A	Lie down for a While at an Urban Oasis in Shanghai ················ 58
	Part B	Living off the Grid ··············· 60
	Part C	A Hygge Way to Happiness ······ 63
	Part D	The Magic of Bookshops ········· 65
	Part E	Projects ································ 66
Unit 7	**Sports** ·· **67**	
	Part A	Health Benefits of Exercising Outdoors ························· 68
	Part B	Five-Year Runner on How the Sport Transformed His Life ····· 70
	Part C	VR Sports ························ 72
	Part D	Dragon Boat Festival—A Blend of Tradition and Competition ········ 74
	Part E	Projects ································ 76

Unit 8 Entertainment 77

Part A Wordle—The Daily Obsession of Millions 78

Part B Conservation Group Fighting to Save Marilyn Monroe's Los Angeles Home 80

Part C Pop-up Exhibition in Hong Kong Marks 50 Years of Bruce Lee's Death 83

Part D Will Unique Popcorn Buckets Bring People Back into Movie Theaters? ... 85

Part E Projects 87

Unit 9 Business 89

Part A The Collapse of the Silicon Valley Bank 90

Part B How Much Income Is Needed to Buy a Home? 93

Part C Chinese Vehicle Manufacturer BYD Unveils New Double-Decker Bus Design 95

Part D Stock Trading Halted After Markets Plunge at Market Open 96

Part E Projects 98

Unit 10 Technology 101

Part A A Legal Loophole of Driverless Cars 102

Part B Are "Digital Humans" the Wave of the Future with AI? 105

Part C How Artificial Intelligence Changes Consumers' Lives? 107

Part D China's AI: Competition or Cooperation? 108

Part E Projects 109

Unit 11 Literature ··········· 111

- **Part A** The "Dan Brown" of Chinese Literature Makes U.S. Debut ············ 112
- **Part B** What If Robert J. Sawyer Writes a Sci-fi Book About China? ······ 114
- **Part C** Tanzania's Abdulrazak Gurnah Wins 2021 Nobel Prize for Literature ··· 116
- **Part D** University Launches Taylor Swift-Inspired Literature Course ····· 118
- **Part E** Projects ················ 119

Unit 12 Nature ············· 121

- **Part A** Fire Season in Australia ········ 122
- **Part B** How Climate Change Is Impacting Antarctica? ····················· 124
- **Part C** Protecting a Forest by Cutting down Christmas Trees ··········· 126
- **Part D** How China's New National Parks Are Protecting Biodiversity? ··· 128
- **Part E** Projects ················ 130

Appendix I Scripts ············· 131
Appendix II Key to Exercises ········· 201

UNIT 1 Education

Part A ChatGPT in the Classroom

Vocabulary Preparation

plagiarism	/ˈpleɪdʒərɪzəm/	n.	the practice of using or copying someone else's idea or work and pretending that you thought of it or created it 剽窃，抄袭
up-close	/ʌpˈkləʊs/	adj.	from a very short distance 近距离的
prompt	/prɒmpt/	n.	a sign on a computer screen that shows that the computer has finished doing sth. and is ready for more instructions 提示符
option	/ˈɒpʃn/	n.	a thing that is or may be chosen 选择；选项
peek	/piːk/	v.	to look at something quickly and secretly because you should not be looking at it 窥视，偷看
plethora	/ˈpleθərə/	n.	excess; an amount that is greater than is needed or can be used 过多，过量
collegiate	/kəˈliːdʒiət/	adj.	relating to a college or its students 大学的，学院的
pen	/pen/	v.	to write sth. 写
perpetuate	/pəˈpetʃueɪt/	v.	to make sth. such as a bad situation, a belief, etc. continue for a long time 使永久化；使持久化；使持续
viable	/ˈvaɪəbl/	adj.	that can be done; that will be successful 可实施的；切实可行的
decipher	/dɪˈsaɪfə(r)/	v.	to succeed in finding the meaning of sth. that is difficult to read or understand 破译；辨认
time capsule	/taɪmˈkæpsʊl/		a container that is filled with objects that people think are typical of the time they are living in. It is buried so that it can be discovered by people in the future. 时间胶囊（收藏具有时代特征的物品）

Notes

1. **ChatGPT** (Chat Generative Pre-trained Transformer) is an AI language model developed by OpenAI, an American artificial intelligence research laboratory consisting of the non-profit OpenAI Incorporated and its for-profit subsidiary corporation OpenAI Limited Partnership. （大语言模型）ChatGPT

Education UNIT 1

2. **Chatbot** is a software application used to conduct an online chat conversation via text or text-to-speech, in lieu of providing direct contact with a live human agent. 聊天机器人

3. **Kentucky** is a state in the east central United States.（美国）肯塔基州

4. **Lexington** is a city in eastern Kentucky, noted for raising thoroughbred horses. 列克星敦（美国肯塔基州东部一城市）

5. **Oregon** is a state in the northwestern United States on the Pacific.（美国）俄勒冈州

Exercise 1

Listen to the news report and get the main idea.

What is the main topic discussed in the news report?

A. The concerns about plagiarism and cheating with the use of AI in schools.

B. The integration of ChatGPT and AI technology in classrooms.

C. The impact of social media on education.

D. The development of new educational curricula.

Exercise 2

Listen to the news report again and fill in the blanks with the exact words or phrases.

George: In our series, The Tech Effect. It's only been a few months since we started hearing about ChatGPT and the AI chatbot is already finding his way in the classrooms. Rebecca Jarvis is back and we're seeing teachers incorporate this technology into their lesson plans.

Rebecca Jarvis: George, this technology is still so new. It comes with plenty of 1. _____ and it raises some very big questions about plagiarism and cheating, which is why some schools have actually banned it. But other schools are now incorporating ChatGPT into their lesson plans and we got an up-close look at how.

Rebecca Jarvis: These fifth-grade students might look like they're doing an average writing assignment (Teacher: Good. What do you think?), but their prompt wasn't created by their teacher. Instead, they chose from ten different options 2. _____ in seconds by ChatGPT, an artificially intelligent chatbot.

Donnie Piercy	(Fifth-Grade Teacher, 2021 Kentucky Teacher of the Year): Like every other educator, I had that concern. Is this something that students are only going to use to cheat? So I started to think about like "Okay, what role is AI, artificial intelligence, going to play in the classroom".
Rebecca Jarvis:	Kentucky Teacher of the Year, Donnie Piercy, let us peek inside his Lexington fifth-grade class where they utilize ChatGPT in a number of ways from grammar exercises like Find the Bot, where students have to guess which paragraph was written by ChatGPT versus their classmates.
Donnie Piercy:	Do any of these jump out, as, like, "Ooh, I'm pretty sure it's not that one"?
Student 1:	For the second one, because they put "who invented 3. _____ of inventions", they should have put "a plethora".
Donnie Piercy:	Oh, interesting 4. _____ there!
Rebecca Jarvis:	...to reading exercises through personalized plays generated in seconds by the program.
Student 2:	In a typical fifth-grade classroom, the door bursts open, and a superhero named Super Potato bursts in.
Student 3:	Fear not citizens, Super Potato is here to save the day!
Donnie Piercy:	So the big thing that I've looked for as a teacher over the last seventeen years is what things I can bring into my lessons that inspire my students to be creative. With AI, with ChatGPT, I've always looked for a way that I can use this tool to inspire my students to become better students to really 5. _____ content.
Rebecca Jarvis:	Many of his students think of it as something that's here to stay.
Girl 1:	So if it keeps on expanding, that's basically typical for what this generation is doing right now.
Boy 1:	I feel like it can evolve a lot over time.
Boy 2:	If you keep AI, like, safe, (it's) going to be really helpful.
Rebecca Jarvis:	And it's not just elementary school. Across the country in Oregon, mother and son teachers Tobin and Cherie Shields utilize it at the high school and 6. _____ level.
Tobin Shields	(Computer Information Systems Instructor): It is going to make

	our educational system more accurate and it's going to make it more interesting and more 7. _____ and more creative, where I think a lot of educators think it's going to do the opposite.
Rebecca Jarvis:	Cherie, an educator of thirty years penning an opinion piece for Education Week titled "Don't ban ChatGPT. Use it as a teaching tool".
Cherie Shield (High School English Teacher):	I do think employers in the future are going to be asking employees to work with AI. It's just a life skill that we are going to have to perpetuate forward if we want our students to be 8. _____ in the workplace.
Rebecca Jarvis:	Some very interesting applications there. But of course, there are those very real concerns about cheating, plagiarism, 9. _____. OpenAI, the company that created ChatGPT has also created what they call an AI Classifier. That is a program that can essentially decipher whether a text was written by AI or by a human. Many other companies are working on similar programs. George, I predict this piece is going to be in a time 10. _____ thirty years from now. Those fifth graders talking about the future. We're going to look at the world so differently because of this technology.
George:	You don't want kids to lose the ability to write.
Rebecca Jarvis:	Exactly and have creativity and come from themselves, not from the machine.
George:	Rebecca, thanks very much.

Part B Future of Education: How Is AI Affecting the Study of the Humanities in China?

Vocabulary Preparation

| cutting-edge | /ˌkʌtɪŋˈedʒ/ | adj. | representing the most advanced stage of development; the newest and most innovative
最先进的；尖端的 |

humanities	/hjuːˈmænətɪz/	n.	(pl.) branches of learning that investigate human culture, such as literature, history, and philosophy 人文学科
elite	/eɪˈliːt/	adj.	consisting of the most powerful, rich, or talented people in a particular group 精英的；杰出的
archaeology	/ˌɑːkiˈɒlədʒi/	n.	the study of human history and prehistory through the excavation of sites and the analysis of artifacts and other physical remains 考古学
outcome	/ˈaʊtkʌm/	n.	the result or consequence of an action or event 结果；后果
museology	/ˌmjuːziˈɒlədʒi/	n.	the study of the organization and methods of museums 博物馆学
ultimately	/ˈʌltɪmətli/	adv.	in the end; finally 最终，最后
verge	/vɜːdʒ/	n.	the point at which sth. is about to happen; the brink 边缘；临界点
quantitative	/ˈkwɒntɪtətɪv/	adj.	relating to or involving the measurement of quantity or amount 定量的
interdisciplinary	/ˌɪntəˈdɪsəplɪnəri/	adj.	involving two or more academic disciplines or fields of study 交叉学科的，跨学科的
intersect	/ˌɪntəˈsekt/	v.	to cross or overlap each other; to have a point or area in common 相交；交叉
autonomously	/ɔːˈtɒnəməsli/	adv.	independently; having the freedom to act or function without external control 自主地；独立地

 Note

CGTN (China Global Television Network) is a global news network that covers China and the world with breaking news, analysis, opinions, culture, sports, and more. 中国国际电视台

Exercise

Listen to the news report and choose the best answer to each of the following questions.

1. What is the main idea of the news report?
   A. The history of AI development.

B. The impact of AI on social media.

C. The ethical issues raised by AI technology.

D. The use of AI in arts and humanities education in China.

2. What can be inferred about the future of AI in archaeological research?

   A. AI will replace human researchers entirely.

   B. AI will become more accessible to students and early career researchers.

   C. AI will only be used for image analysis.

   D. AI will make archaeological research more difficult.

3. According to Zhang Hai, what is one benefit of AI in archeology?

   A. It eliminates the need for human logic in research.

   B. It provides immediate results for pattern matching.

   C. It replaces the need for quantitative archeology.

   D. It makes spatial analysis unnecessary.

4. What new opportunities are being created for philosophy majors according to the news report?

   A. Opportunities in AI ethics outside the university.

   B. Opportunities in AI development.

   C. Opportunities in archaeological research.

   D. Opportunities in social media management.

5. What is the role of the Artificial Intelligence Research Institute at Peking University?

   A. To develop AI that can act autonomously based on correct values.

   B. To focus solely on the technological aspects of AI.

   C. To replace traditional humanities education with AI.

   D. To limit the use of AI to the field of social media.

 Part C   No Smartphones on Campus

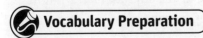

| tight-knit | /ˌtaɪtˈnɪt/ | adj. | closely connected and well-organized 紧密团结的；关系紧密的 |

be glued to			to be giving all your attention to sth., especially a screen or device 全神贯注于（尤指屏幕或设备）
discreetly	/dɪˈskriːtli/	adv.	in a careful and prudent manner, especially in order to keep sth. confidential or to avoid embarrassment 谨慎地；悄悄地
scroll	/skrəʊl/	v.	to move text or images on a computer screen in order to view different parts of them 滚动（屏幕上的文本或图像）
the jury is still out			used to say that a decision has not yet been made on a controversial or doubtful matter（某事）尚未有定论
overrate	/ˌəʊvəˈreɪt/	v.	to have too high an opinion of sth./sb. 对……评价过高

Notes

1. **Massachusetts** is a state in the New England region of the northeastern United States. It is known for its significant colonial history, prestigious universities such as Harvard and MIT, and its diverse cultural heritage. 马萨诸塞州（美国东北部新英格兰地区的一个州）

2. **CNN** (Cable News Network) is an American news-based pay television channel launched in 1980. It was the first television channel to provide 24-hour news coverage and the first all-news television channel in the United States.（美国有线电视新闻网）CNN

Exercise

Listen to the news report and decide whether the following statements are true (T) or false (F).

1. All the students at Buxton School live full-time in the school campus. (   )
2. After the smartphone ban, some students felt more socially connected with their peers. (   )
3. The ban on smartphones at Buxton School led to an increase of student participation in the black and white photography program. (   )
4. Students at Buxton School were initially happy about the smartphone ban. (   )
5. After the smartphone ban, students were no longer allowed to use any electronic devices, including iPads and computers. (   )

Education 1 UNIT

 Part D   Tuition-Free

 Vocabulary Preparation

studio	/ˈstjuːdiəʊ/	n.	a room where music, radio, or television programs are recorded or broadcast 录音室；广播室；演播室
total	/ˈtəʊtl/	v.	to reach a particular amount or number 总数达；共计
reimburse	/ˌriːɪmˈbɜːs/	v.	to pay back money to sb. which he or she has spent or lost 偿还；补偿
board of trustees			a governing board elected or appointed to direct the policies of an educational institution（大学）董事会
rehabilitation	/ˌriːəˌbɪlɪˈteɪʃn/	n.	the treatment of physical disabilities by massage and electrotherapy and exercises 康复；恢复
screening	/ˈskriːnɪŋ/	n.	the testing or examining of a large number of people or things for disease, faults, etc. 筛查
late	/leɪt/	adj.	(of a person) no longer alive 已故的；已逝的
protege	/ˈprɒtəʒeɪ/	n.	(from French) a young person who is helped in his or her career and personal development by a more experienced person 受提携的后进；门徒

 Notes

1. **Albert Einstein College of Medicine** is a private, research-intensive medical school in New York City. Founded in 1953, Einstein operates as an independent degree-granting institution. 阿尔伯特·爱因斯坦医学院

2. **Bronx** is one of the five boroughs of New York City, the northernmost one. 布朗克斯区（纽约五个行政区中最北面的一个区）

3. **Ruth Gottesman** (1930–) is a long-time professor and the chair of the board of trustees of the Albert Einstein College of Medicine in New York, who donated $1 billion in 2024 to the college to ensure that tuition would be free in perpetuity to all future students. 露丝·戈特曼

4. **Berkshire Hathaway** is an American holding company based in Omaha, Nebraska, led by billionaire investor Warren Buffett. It owns dozens of companies across various sectors and industries, including insurance, utilities, energy. 伯克希尔·哈撒韦公司

5. **Warren Buffett** (1930–) is an American businessman, investor, and philanthropist who currently serves as the co-founder, chairman, and CEO of Berkshire Hathaway. 沃伦·巴菲特

Exercise

Listen to the news report and answer the following questions.

1. How will the $1 billion donation specifically benefit current and future students at the Albert Einstein College of Medicine?
2. What motivated Ruth Gottesman to make the $1 billion donation to the Albert Einstein College of Medicine, and how did her professional background contribute to this decision?
3. What role do you think Ruth Gottesman's late husband, David, and his association with Warren Buffett might have played in shaping her philanthropic vision and actions?
4. What are the potential social and economic impacts of making medical education tuition-free at Albert Einstein College of Medicine?
5. What are the broader implications for medical education and healthcare if other institutions follow the example set by Ruth Gottesman and the Albert Einstein College of Medicine?

Part E Projects

Choose one of the following projects, or design one of your own, concerning the theme of this unit. Finish the project by giving a presentation on it in class and chairing a discussion afterwards.

1. Investigate how AI technologies like ChatGPT are being integrated into classrooms in China. Discuss the benefits and potential drawbacks of using AI in education, and provide specific examples and case studies to support your points. Conclude with your opinion on whether AI should play a larger role in education.
2. Design your vision of the ideal future classroom. Consider the role of AI, the use of technology, classroom policies such as smartphone bans, and the financial aspects of education. Create a detailed plan and present it to your classmates, explaining how each element contributes to a better learning environment.

3. Investigate the concept of tuition-free education by examining some examples of countries or institutions that have implemented this model. Discuss the benefits and challenges of providing tuition-free education. Present your findings and argue whether it is a viable solution for improving access to education.

UNIT 2 People

Part A Martin Luther King's Legacy

Vocabulary Preparation

rededicate	/ˌriːˈdedɪkeɪt/	v.	to give a lot of one's time and effort to a particular activity or purpose again; to dedicate anew 重新投入；再次奉献
resonate	/ˈrezəneɪt/	v.	to have a special meaning or when it is particularly important to sb.; to remind sb. of sth. 有特殊意义；引起共鸣
converge	/kənˈvɜːdʒ/	v.	(of different ideas or societies) to stop being different and become similar to each other 趋同；融合
pilgrimage	/ˈpɪlɡrɪmɪdʒ/	n.	a journey that sb. makes to a place that is very important to him or her; a journey to a sacred place 重要旅程；朝圣
culminate	/ˈkʌlmɪneɪt/	v.	to end, especially to reach a final or climactic stage or with a particular result 告终；结束
spectacle	/ˈspektəkl/	n.	a performance or an event that is very impressive and exciting to look at 精彩的表演；壮观的场面
grapple	/ˈɡræpl/	v.	to try hard to solve a problem or difficulty 努力解决（问题）；设法克服（困难）
drawn	/drɔːn/	adj.	looking pale, very tired, ill, worried, or unhappy 憔悴的；苍白的；愁眉苦脸的
at stake			that can be won or lost, depending on the success of a particular action 成败难料；有风险
oratory	/ˈɒrətri/	n.	the art of making formal speeches which strongly affect people's feelings and beliefs 演讲术；雄辩术
sermon	/ˈsɜːmən/	n.	a talk on a moral or religious subject; moral advice that a person tries to give in a long talk 布道；冗长的说教
piercing	/ˈpɪəsɪŋ/	adj.	loud and sharp, affecting the feelings strongly 打动人心的
biting	/ˈbaɪtɪŋ/	adj.	cruel and critical 刻薄的；辛辣的
indict	/ɪnˈdaɪt/	v.	to accuse formally of a crime 控告；起诉
emancipation	/ɪˌmænsɪˈpeɪʃn/	n.	freeing from unpleasant or unfair social, political, or legal restrictions 解放；摆脱束缚

People 2 UNIT

proclamation	/ˌprɒkləˈmeɪʃn/	n.	an official statement about sth. important that is made to the public; the act of making an official statement 宣言；公告
manacle	/ˈmænəkl/	n.	a metal device attached to a prisoner's wrists or legs in order to prevent him or her from moving or escaping 镣铐
hallowed	/ˈhæləʊd/	adj.	holy; respected and admired 神圣的；受崇敬的；受尊崇的
haunt	/hɔːnt/	v.	to keep thinking or worrying about sth. unpleasant over a long period of time 萦绕心头；难以忘却；缠绕

 Notes

1. **Martin Luther King Jr.** (1929–1968) was an American social activist and political philosopher who was one of the most prominent leaders in the Civil Rights Movement from 1955 until his assassination in 1968. 马丁·路德·金
2. **Pierre Thomas** (1954–) is an American journalist. He serves as senior justice correspondent at ABC News. 皮埃尔·托马斯
3. **The Civil Rights Movement** was a social movement and campaign from 1954 to 1968 in the United States to abolish legalized racial segregation, discrimination, and disenfranchisement in the country.（美国黑人）民权运动（20 世纪 50—60 年代非裔美国人争取平等权利的运动）
4. **Lincoln Memorial** is a U.S. national memorial built to honor the 16th president of the United States, Abraham Lincoln. 林肯纪念堂
5. **Georgia** is a state in the southeastern United States.（美国）佐治亚州
6. ***This Week*** is an American Sunday morning political affairs program on the ABC television network.（美国 ABC 新闻政论节目）《本周》

Exercise 1

Listen to the news report and get the main idea.

What is the main point of the news report?

A. Yolanda Renee King felt so proud to have the chance to speak today as the grandchild of Martin Luther King Jr.

B. The Civil Rights Movement in America has already made great progress 60 years after King's famous inspiring speech.

C. What King has said in his speech 60 years ago still resonates today, inspiring black Americans to continue to fight against the manacles of segregation and the chains of discrimination.

D. Despite the political aggressive and piercing words of King in his speech, many Americans still believe his sweeping oratory to be more like a sermon.

Exercise 2

Listen to the news report again and fill in the blanks with the exact words or phrases.

Yolanda Renee King: If I could speak to my grandfather today, I would say I'm sorry we still have to be here, to rededicate ourselves to finishing your work and ultimately realizing your 1. _____ .

Martha: That was Dr. Martin Luther King Jr.'s only grandchild, 15-year-old Yolanda Renee King, marking the 60th anniversary of the March on Washington this weekend. ABC's chief justice correspondent Pierre Thomas reflects on King's most famous speech and why his dream still 2. _____ today.

Martin Luther King: I have a dream that one day…

Pierre Thomas: Sixty years ago, the hopes and, yes, dreams of the Civil Rights Movement converged in what was truly a historic moment as the pilgrimage of 250,000 people culminated on the National Mall at the feet of the Lincoln Memorial. The country had never seen anything quite like this—a(n) 3. _____ of consequence involving a nation grappling with race, freedom, issues of class and simple human dignity. What would King have to say that day? Would there be violence? How would police react? How would the nation respond? The fact that there were 6,000 National Guardsmen and nearly as many D.C. police 4. _____ tells you everything you need to know. But why is it that all these years later we pause to remember and ask the young to study that day? What is it? Why are we still 5. _____? Why can't we let that day go? Why mustn't we let it go? Perhaps it is because what was 6. _____, because we know right now the journey towards a more perfect union is far from over. But the answer lies in King's speech, undoubtedly one of the most important in the nation's history. Many remember the 7. _____, hopeful, spiritual oratory of what at times seems more like a sermon.

Martin Luther King: I have a dream that one day, on the red hills of Georgia, sons of former slaves and the sons of former 8. _____, will be able to sit down together at the table of brotherhood.

Pierre Thomas: But King's words that day were also political, aggressive, piercing, even biting. He was demanding action and indicting the country. The speech begins with a(n) 9. _____ to the Emancipation Proclamation, and how it freed slaves, but within forty words, King has this to say—

Martin Luther King: But 100 years later, the Negro still is not free. One hundred years later, the life of the Negro is still sadly 10. _____ by the manacles of segregation and the chains of discrimination.

Pierre Thomas: And later this—

Martin Luther King: We have also come to this hallowed spot to remind America of the fierce urgency of now.

Pierre Thomas: King rose to the moment, spoke to the moment in a speech that inspires us, motivates us, and, yes, haunts us to this very day. For *This Week*, Pierre Thomas, ABC News, Washington.

Martha: Our thanks to our Pierre Thomas for those important reflections.

Part B   Henry Kissinger Died at 100

 Vocabulary Preparation

renowned	/rɪˈnaʊnd/	adj.	famous and respected 有名的；闻名的；受尊敬的
diplomat	/ˈdɪpləmæt/	n.	a person whose job is to represent his or her country in a foreign country, for example, in an embassy 外交官
stalwart	/ˈstɔːlwət/	n.	a loyal supporter who does a lot of work for an organization, especially a political party（政党等组织的）忠诚拥护者；坚定分子
conceivable	/kənˈsiːvəbl/	adj.	possible; that you can imagine or believe 可想象的；可信的
escalate	/ˈeskəleɪt/	v.	to become or make sth. greater, worse, more serious, etc. 升级；不断恶化；加剧
orchestrate	/ˈɔːkɪstreɪt/	v.	to organize a complicated plan or event very carefully or secretly 精心安排；策划

 Notes

1. **Henry Kissinger** (1923–2023) is an American diplomat, political scientist, geopolitical consultant, and politician who served as United States Secretary of State and National Security Advisor under the presidential administrations of Richard Nixon and Gerald Ford. 亨利·基辛格

2. **George Stephanopoulos** (1961–) is an American television host and political commentator. He has anchored ABC's *This Week* since 2012, after first hosting it from 2002 to 2010. 乔治·史蒂芬诺普洛斯

3. **President Kennedy** (John F. Kennedy) (1917–1963) is an American politician who served as the 35th president of the United States from 1961 until his assassination in 1963. 肯尼迪总统

4. **President Johnson** (Lyndon B. Johnson) (1908–1973) is an American politician who served as the 36th president of the United States from 1963 to 1969. 约翰逊总统

5. **President Richard Nixon** (1913–1994) is the 37th president of the United States, serving from 1969 to 1974. 理查德·尼克松总统

6. **Soviet Union** is a former communist country in eastern Europe and northern Asia.

Unit 2 People

Established in 1922 and officially dissolved on 31 December, 1991, it included Russia and 14 other soviet socialist republics at that time. 苏联

7. **The Vietnam War** is a conflict in Vietnam, Laos, and Cambodia from 1 November, 1955 to the fall of Saigon on 30 April, 1975. 越南战争

8. **Cambodia** is a nation in southeastern Asia. 柬埔寨

9. **Watergate Scandal** is a major political scandal in the United States, involving the administration of President Richard Nixon from 1972 to 1974 that led to Nixon's resignation. 水门事件

10. **President Gerald Ford** (1913–2006) is an American politician who served as the 38th president of the United States from 1974 to 1977. 杰拉尔德·福特总统

11. **Ukraine** is a country in southeastern Europe. 乌克兰

12. **Volodymyr Zelenskyy** (1978–) is a Ukrainian politician who has been serving as the sixth president of Ukraine since 2019. 弗拉基米尔·泽连斯基

Exercise

Listen to the news report and choose the best answer to each of the following statements or questions.

1. According to the news report, Kissinger _____.
   A. had served many American presidents including President Kennedy
   B. had won a Nobel Peace Prize
   C. had helped America shape its foreign policy for decades
   D. all of the above

2. According to the news report, which of the following is NOT true about Henry Kissinger?
   A. Kissinger was one of the most influential and controversial politicians in America.
   B. Kissinger served as the Foreign Policy Advisor for President Kennedy on a part-time basis.
   C. Kissinger was a Jewish refugee from Greece.
   D. Kissinger was named National Security Advisor by President Nixon.

3. Which of the following is NOT the title Henry Kissinger used to hold?
   A. Winner of the Presidential Medal of Freedom.
   B. Winner of the Nobel Prize in Economics.

C. Professor of Harvard University.

D. The U.S. Secretary of State.

4. How old was Henry Kissinger when he came to the United States of America?

   A. 4.　　　　B. 15.　　　　C. 43.　　　　D. 14.

5. Henry Kissinger had played a major role in _____.

   A. the restoration of U.S.-China relations

   B. escalation of the Vietnam War

   C. the relaxation of the U.S.-Soviet Union tensions

   D. all of the above

Part C　Queen Elizabeth II Died at 96

Vocabulary Preparation

majesty	/ˈmædʒəsti/	n.	a title of respect used when speaking about or to a king or queen（对国王或女王的尊称）陛下
succession	/səkˈseʃn/	n.	the act of taking over an official position or title; the right to take over an official position or title, especially to become the king or queen of a country 继任；继承（权）
condolence	/kənˈdəʊləns/	n.	sympathy that you feel for sb. when a person in his or her family or that he or she knows well has died; an expression of this sympathy 吊唁，慰唁
unmatched	/ˌʌnˈmætʃt/	adj.	better than all others 无双的；无比的
constancy	/ˈkɒnstənsi/	n.	the quality of being faithful 忠诚，忠实
bedrock	/ˈbedrɒk/	n.	a strong base for sth., especially the facts or the principles on which it is based 牢固基础
stalwart	/ˈstɔːlwət/	adj.	loyal, steady, and completely reliable 忠实的；坚定的；完全可靠的
outpouring	/ˈaʊtpɔːrɪŋ/	n.	a strong and sudden expression of feeling（感情的）迸发；倾泻
protocol	/ˈprəʊtəkɒl/	n.	a system of fixed rules and formal behavior used at official meetings, usually between governments 礼仪；外交礼节

sovereign	/ˈsɒvrɪn/	n.	a king or queen 君主；元首
cane	/keɪn/	n.	a piece of thin stick, used to help sb. to walk 手杖
monarch	/ˈmɒnək/	n.	a person who rules a country, for example a king or queen 君主，帝王
episodic	/ˌepɪˈsɒdɪk/	adj.	happening occasionally and not at regular intervals 偶发的
platinum	/ˈplætɪnəm/	n.	a silver-grey precious chemical metal element, used in making expensive jewellery and in industry 铂；白金
jubilee	/ˈdʒuːbɪliː/	n.	a special anniversary of an event, especially the 25th or 50th anniversary; the celebrations connected with it. Among monarchies, it usually refers to a 70th anniversary.（尤指25周年或50周年的，皇室一般指70周年）周年（纪念），周年庆祝
frail	/freɪl/	adj.	(especially of an old person) physically weak and thin（尤指老人）瘦弱的
reign	/reɪn/	n.	the period during which a king, queen, emperor, etc. rules 君主统治时期

Notes

1. **Queen Elizabeth II** (1926–2022) was Queen of the United Kingdom and other Commonwealth realms from 1952 until her death in 2022. Her reign of 70 years and 214 days is the longest of any British monarch or female monarch.（英国女王）伊丽莎白二世

2. **Buckingham Palace** is a royal residence in London, and the administrative headquarters of the monarch of the United Kingdom. 白金汉宫

3. **Commonwealth** is an organization consisting of the United Kingdom and most of the countries that used to be part of the British Empire. 英联邦（由英国和大多数曾经隶属于大英帝国的国家组成）

4. **Charles** (Charles Philip Arthur George) (1948–) is the former title of Charles III, King of the United Kingdom and other Commonwealth realms.（英王）查尔斯

5. **Prince William** (William Arthur Philip Louis) (1982–) is the heir apparent to the British throne. He is the elder son of King Charles III and Diana, Princess of Wales. 威廉王子

6. **Prince George** (George Alexander Louis) (2013–) is a member of the British royal family. He is the eldest child of William, Prince of Wales, and Catherine, Princess of Wales. 乔治王子

7. **President Biden** (Joseph Robinette Biden Jr.) (1942–) is an American politician who served as the 46th president of the United States from 2021 to 2025. 拜登总统

8. **Charlie D'Agata** (1970–) is a senior foreign reporter from CBS News based in the London Bureau since 2011. 查理·达加塔

9. **Norah O'Donnell** (1974–) is an American television journalist who is the anchor of the CBS Evening News, a correspondent for *60 Minutes*, and host of *Person to Person*. 诺拉·奥唐纳

10. **Kate** (Catherine Elizabeth Middleton) (1982–) is a member of the British royal family. She is married to William, Prince of Wales, heir apparent to the British throne. 凯特王妃

11. **Prince Harry** (Henry Charles Albert David) (1984–) is a member of the British royal family, the younger son of King Charles III. 哈里王子

12. **Megan** (Rachel Meghan Markle) (1981–) is a former American actress and the wife of Prince Harry. 梅根（哈里王子的妻子）

13. **Balmoral Castle** is a large estate house in Scotland, and a residence of the British royal family. 巴尔莫勒尔堡

14. **Liz Truss** (1975–) is a British politician who served as Prime Minister of the United Kingdom and leader of the Conservative Party from September to October 2022. 利兹·特拉斯

15. **Prince Philip** (1921–2021) was the husband of Queen Elizabeth II. 菲利普亲王

> **Exercise**
>
> *Listen to the news report and decide whether the following statements are true (T) or false (F).*
>
> 1. At the very last moment of her life in her summer home in Balmoral Castle, Queen Elizabeth II was accompanied by her sons and their families. (   )
>
> 2. The royal line of succession indicates that the nine-year old Prince George will be the third successor in the wake of the Queen's death. (   )
>
> 3. Liz Truss, the new Prime Minister of the U.K., said the nation was devastated at the loss of the 96-year-old monarch who had given her an audience just two days ago. (   )

4. The whole country, even the world, is greatly grief-stricken at the news, profoundly mourning the loss of the beloved sovereign of United Kingdom and the great international figure. (   )
5. Prince Charles, who automatically became the King after the passing of the Queen, will be fully responsible for the funeral arrangements of his mother. (   )

Part D   Zhang Guimei, a Dedicated People's Teacher

Vocabulary Preparation

backward	/ˈbækwəd/	adj.	having made less progress than normal; developing slowly 落后的；进步缓慢的
convene	/kənˈviːn/	v.	to arrange for people to come together for a formal meeting 召集；召开（正式会议）
solemnity	/səˈlemnəti/	n.	the quality of being very serious and dignified 庄严；庄重
sacredness	/ˈseɪkrɪdnəs/	n.	the quality of being important and respectful 受尊重；受崇敬
go all out			to make a very great effort to get sth. or do sth. 全力以赴
intake	/ˈɪnteɪk/	n.	the number of people who are allowed to enter a school, college, profession, etc. during a particular period（一定时期内）纳入的人数；新招收者
perseverance	/ˌpɜːsɪˈvɪərəns/	n.	the quality of continuing to try to achieve a particular aim despite difficulties 毅力；韧性；不屈不挠的精神

Notes

1. **Zhang Guimei** (1957–) is a Chinese educator who is the founder and principal of Huaping High School for Girls, China's first and only free public high school for girls in a poor, mountainous region in southwest China's Yunnan Province. 张桂梅
2. **Jiao Yulu** (1922–1964) is a symbol of the honest Party cadre who devoted himself tirelessly to the country. As Party chief of Lankao County in Henan Province, Jiao Yulu mobilized the people to combat the poor natural conditions. 焦裕禄

Exercise

Listen to the news report and answer the following questions.

1. Why was Zhang Guimei listed as one of the top ten people that moved China in 2020?
2. Why was Zhang Guimei determined to build a free senior high school for girls in the mountains?
3. What had happened to the faculty six months after the establishment of the school?
4. How did Zhang Guimei solve the problem of high turnover rate?
5. How many girls have their fate changed after twelve years of perseverance?

Part E Projects

Choose one of the following projects, or design one of your own, concerning the theme of this unit. Finish the project by giving a presentation on it in class and chairing a discussion afterwards.

1. Search the Internet and download the video of the speech *I Have a Dream* by Martin Luther King Jr. Watch and study the video carefully and do a dubbing in class.

2. Search the Internet to learn more about the roles the royal family has played in the U.K. Explore the lives of both minor and major royals, and evaluate whether it would be beneficial to abolish the monarchy. Prepare a presentation to share your views in class.

3. Conduct a survey to identify an outstanding and respected figure in China. Prepare a report on this person and present it to your class, followed by leading a discussion.

UNIT 3 Food

Part A The Ultimate Chinese Food Tour—Peking Duck in Beijing

Vocabulary Preparation

immersed	/ɪˈmɜːst/	adj.	completely involved in sth. 沉浸的；深陷的
cuisine	/kwɪˈziːn/	n.	a style of cooking that is characteristic of a place 烹饪；风味
embedded	/ɪmˈbedɪd/	adj.	fixed firmly into sth. else 嵌入的；融入的
specialty	/ˈspeʃəlti/	n.	a special food or product that is always very good in a place 特色食品；特产
scallion	/ˈskæliən/	n.	a small onion with long green leaves 青葱
bon appétit			（法语）好胃口
crunchy	/ˈkrʌntʃi/	adj.	firm and crisp and making a sharp sound when you bite or crush it 松脆的
utilize	/ˈjuːtəlaɪz/	v.	to use sth., especially for a practical purpose 使用；应用
intangible	/ɪnˈtændʒəbl/	adj.	abstract or hard to define or measure 非物质的；无形的
inheritor	/ɪnˈherɪtə(r)/	n.	a person who is affected by the work, ideas, etc. of people who lived before them 传承人
roast	/rəʊst/	n.	the cooking of food, especially meat, without liquid in an oven or over a fire 烤肉
radiate	/ˈreɪdieɪt/	v.	to send out heat in all directions 散发（热量）
tender	/ˈtendə(r)/	adj.	(of food) easy to bite through and cut （食物）嫩的
crispy	/ˈkrɪspi/	adj.	(of food) pleasantly hard and dry （食物）酥脆的
secure	/sɪˈkjʊə(r)/	v.	to obtain or achieve sth., especially when this means using a lot of effort （尤指经过努力）获得；取得
smoky	/ˈsməʊki/	adj.	tasting or smelling like smoke 有烟熏味的
time-honored	/ˈtaɪmˈɒnəd/	adj.	of long standing and acceptance; long-established 古老的；传统的
craving	/ˈkreɪvɪŋ/	n.	a strong desire for sth. 强烈的愿望；渴望

Unit 3 Food

 Notes

1. **Bianyifang** is one of the time-honored and most famous roast duck restaurants in Beijing. Established in the Yongle Period in the Ming Dynasty, it has a history of more than 600 years, and is representative of the closed-oven type, with ducks roasted without using an open fire. 便宜坊（烤鸭）

2. **China's Intangible Cultural Heritage List** encompasses oral traditions, performing arts, social practices, and knowledge and skills surrounding traditional crafts in China. It is culture rooted in community, passed down from generation to generation and adapted to remain relevant in today's society. 中国非物质文化遗产目录

3. **Quanjude**, established in 1864 during the Qing Dynasty, is famous for its time-honored method of roasting the duck. The ducks are cooked in specially designed wood-fired ovens, and have a tender, juicy flavor. 全聚德（烤鸭）

Exercise 1

Listen to the news report and get the main idea.

What is the main point of the news report?

A. Closed-oven Peking Duck from Bianyifang.

B. Open-oven Peking Duck from Quanjude.

C. Peking Duck roasting traditions and flavors.

D. Where to satisfy your Peking Duck craving.

Exercise 2

Listen to the news report again and fill in the blanks with the exact words or phrases.

Walking through the streets of Beijing, you're immersed in the sights and smells of local cuisine. But one dish is so embedded in the city's **1.** _____ that it even bears its name.

Host: I'd like Peking Duck, please. Thanks.

Yes, Peking Duck. As early as in Yuan Dynasty (1271–1368), this mouth-watering **2.** _____ has been a local favorite and no trip to the capital is complete without a taste.

Host: This is what I've been waiting. Flour pancake here. This is the Peking Duck that was freshly cut, gonna dip into this sweet and savory sauce we have, next step, cucumbers, and then we have scallions here. Alright, bon appétit. Ah. It's so good. You can taste the meat—it's kind of **3.** _____ on the outside—and then the sauce is sweet, mixes with the cucumbers. It's like a birthday present for your mouth.

The duck I'm eating now was cooked by Bianyifang. The 600-year-old restaurant uses a(n) **4.** _____ technique that doesn't utilize an open flame. The method is cherished enough to have a spot on China's **5.** _____ Cultural Heritage List. Bai Yongming is the inheritor of the cooking style and has been practicing his craft for 40 years.

Host: So I just tried the Peking Duck upstairs and now I kind of want to see the background about how it's made.

Bai Yongming: [Dialog in Chinese...] Although the Peking Duck tastes good, the cooking process is quite complex. First, we would use Beijing-local stuffed ducks that are 39 to 41 days old. Each duck weighs between 3 kg and 3.1 kg. Before the roast begins, the duck needs to be stuffed and then we pour soup in it.

Host: Okay.

Ducks are filled with a special soup and hung inside the oven where the heat **6.** _____ from the inner walls produces a tender result.

Bai Yongming: Yes, yes, let's do it.

While Bianyifang sticks to its tradition of closed-oven roasting, just down the street, Quanjude does things a little **7.** _____. Quanjude traces its history back to 1864 during the Qing Dynasty (1644–1911). The restaurant specializes in an open-oven roasting style, where ducks are hung over a flame fueled by wood from **8.** _____, giving it a slightly crispy skin without sacrificing taste. Their unique style has also **9.** _____ a spot on China's Intangible Cultural Heritage List.

Host: Inside the kitchen, the way they cook the duck here is very different from Bianyifang. It's cooked in the open oven. There's actually wood inside of it, which gives it a slightly smoky taste when you try it, and the skin is slightly crispy, but the same amazing taste.

I've tried two unique styles of Peking Duck, both using time-honored traditions to produce tasty results. So, whether you choose Bianyifang or Quanjude, the next time you have a Peking Duck 10. _____, you're almost certain to have a meal worth remembering.

Host: That's good. That's good.

Part B Study Finds Highly Processed Foods Linked to Early Death

Vocabulary Preparation

pretzel	/'pretsl/	n.	a crispy salty biscuit in the shape of a knot or stick, often served with drinks at a party 椒盐卷饼
flavoring	/'fleɪvərɪŋ/	n.	sth. added to food primarily for the savor it imparts 调味品
additive	/'ædətɪv/	n.	a substance that is added in small amounts in sth., especially food, in order to improve it, give it color, make it last longer, etc.（食品）添加剂
attributable	/ə'trɪbjətəbl/	adj.	probably caused by the thing mentioned 可归因于；可能由于
diabetes	/ˌdaɪə'biːtiːz/	n.	a medical condition in which sb. has too much sugar in his or her blood 糖尿病
considerable	/kən'sɪdərəbl/	adj.	great in amount, size, importance, etc. 相当多的
sparingly	/'speərɪŋli/	adv.	carefully to use or give only a little of sth. 慎用地
if at all			used to give emphasis 就算真的有，也……（置于句末，具体意思根据句子前半部分而定）
cohort	/'kəʊhɔːt/	n.	(technical) a group of people who share a common feature or aspect of behavior 同龄组；一批人
moderation	/ˌmɒdə'reɪʃn/	n.	the quality of being reasonable and not being extreme 适度，适中

Notes

1. **Ultra-processed foods** refer to foods that have been altered to include fats, starches,

sugars, salts, hydrogenated oils, etc. All of these additions add taste and flavor, and make the foods shelf-stable. However, they also have negative health implications. 超加工食品

2. **NBC** (National Broadcasting Co.) is a major American broadcast network that offers a variety of programs, including news, sports, comedy, drama, and reality shows. （美国）全国广播公司

3. *American Journal of Clinical Nutrition* is a highly rated peer-reviewed, primary research journal in nutrition and dietetics. This journal publishes the latest research on topics in nutrition, such as obesity, vitamins and minerals, nutrition and disease, and energy metabolism which are relevant to human and clinical nutrition. 《美国临床营养学杂志》

Exercise

Listen to the news report and choose the best answer to each of the following statements or questions.

1. Ultra-processed foods are NOT rich in _____.
   A. flavorings B. additives
   C. preservatives D. whole ingredients

2. Which of the following is NOT an example of ultra-processed foods?
   A. Chips. B. Yogurt.
   C. Pretzels. D. Hot dogs.

3. The new study found that more than _____ of those early deaths were attributable to ultra-processed foods.
   A. 10% B. 20%
   C. 30% D. 40%

4. The *American Journal of Clinical Nutrition* said that ultra-processed foods make up about _____ of the daily calories in the U.S.
   A. 100% B. 85%
   C. 75% D. 50%

5. What's Ari Bendix, the health reporter's suggestion regarding ultra-processed foods?
   A. Give up these foods entirely.
   B. Eat pizza twice in the weekend.
   C. Cut back these foods by half in your diet.
   D. Scale back these foods to a quarter of your diet.

Part C   Seawater Rice—A Solution for Global Food Security

Vocabulary Preparation

anniversary	/ˌænɪˈvɜːsəri/	n.	a date that is an exact number of years after a date of important or special event 周年纪念日
underestimate	/ˌʌndəˈestɪmeɪt/	v.	to think or guess that the amount, cost, or size of sth. is smaller than it really is 低估；轻视
sustainable	/səˈsteɪnəbl/	adj.	that can continue or be continued for a long time 可持续的
dimension	/daɪˈmenʃn/	n.	an aspect, or way of looking at or thinking about sth. 方面；侧面；维度
availability	/əˌveɪləˈbɪləti/	n.	(of things) that you can get, buy, or find 可获得性
transformation	/ˌtrænsfəˈmeɪʃn/	n.	a complete change in sth.（彻底的）变化；改观
recipient	/rɪˈsɪpiənt/	n.	a person who receives sth. 受方；接受者
donor	/ˈdəʊnə(r)/	n.	a person or an organization that makes a gift of money, clothes, food, etc. to a charity, etc. 捐赠者
malnourished	/ˌmælˈnʌrɪʃt/	adj.	in bad health because of a lack of food or a lack of the right type of food 营养不良的
cultivate	/ˈkʌltɪveɪt/	v.	to grow plants or crops 种植；培育
yield	/jiːld/	v.	to produce or provide sth., for example a profit, result, or crop 出产（作物）
hectare	/ˈhekteə(r)/	n.	a measurement of an area of land which is equal to 10,000 square meters 公顷（等于1万平方米）
paramount	/ˈpærəmaʊnt/	adj.	more important than anything else 至为重要的
livelihood	/ˈlaɪvlihʊd/	n.	a means of earning money in order to live 赚钱谋生的手段；生计

agronomist	/əˈgrɒnəmɪst/	n.	a scientist who studies the relationship between crops and the environment 农学家
Saline-Alkali Tolerant Rice (or seawater rice)			耐盐碱水稻（又称海水稻）
tidal flat			海边滩涂；潮滩
barren alkali soil			贫瘠的盐碱地
arable	/ˈærəbl/	adj.	connected with growing crops such as wheat 耕作的，可耕的
genotype	/ˈdʒenətaɪp/	n.	the combination of genes that a particular living thing carries, some of which may not be noticed from its appearance 基因型

Notes

1. **Yuan Longping** (1930–2021) is renowned as the father of hybrid rice. Yuan had devoted his whole life to the research of hybrid rice and the development of genetic materials and technologies essential for breeding high-yielding hybrid rice varieties. His pioneering research helped transform China's food deficiency to food security within three decades. 袁隆平

2. **The Medal of Republic** honors people who made exceptional contributions to the development of the People's Republic of China. The medal has illustrations of China's national emblem, a five-pointed star, the Yellow River, the Yangtze River, a mountain and orchid flowers. 共和国勋章

3. **Zero Hunger** means ending hunger, food insecurity, and malnutrition by 2030, as part of the UN's Sustainable Development Goals. 零饥饿

4. **The Food and Agriculture Organization (FAO)** is a specialized agency of the United Nations that leads international efforts to defeat hunger. FAO's goal is to achieve food security for all and make sure that people have regular access to enough high-quality food to lead active, healthy lives. 联合国粮农组织

5. **The World Food Program (WFP)** is the world's largest humanitarian organization saving lives in emergencies and using food assistance to build a pathway to peace, stability, and prosperity, for people recovering from conflict, disasters, and the impact of climate change. 联合国世界粮食计划署

6. **Hybrid rice** is a type of rice that has been bred from two very different parents. It

can significantly out-yield other rice varieties, and thus, it is a key technology that meets the increasing global demand for rice. 杂交水稻

7. **A community of shared future for mankind** is a concept put forward by the Chinese government to promote global cooperation and development. It emphasizes the interconnectedness and interdependence of all countries and calls for joint efforts to tackle global challenges and achieve common development. 人类命运共同体

Exercise

Listen to the news report and decide whether the following statements are true (T) or false (F).

1. Yuan Longping was awarded China's highest honor—the Medal of Republic—for his contribution to the nation's food security, the development of agricultural science, and global food supply. (   )
2. Due to China's transformation from a major aid recipient to a leading aid donor to the World Food Program, the world will definitely achieve the sustainable development goal of Zero Hunger by 2030. (   )
3. Yuan Longping is not only the father of hybrid rice, but also is leading the research and development of seawater rice. (   )
4. Alkali soils include tidal flats, desert areas, and arable lands. (   )
5. If the seawater rice technology were promoted globally through international collaboration, we would be doing our part to solve the issue of global food security. (   )

Part D Future Food—The Menu of 2030

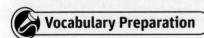

tweak	/twiːk/	v.	to make slight changes to a machine, system, etc. to improve it 稍稍调整；微调
critter	/ˈkrɪtə(r)/	n.	a regional term for creature 生物；动物
earthling	/ˈɜːθlɪŋ/	n.	a word used in science fiction stories by creatures from other planets to refer to a person living on the earth 地球人（科幻小说中外星人用语）

consume	/kən'sjuːm/	v.	to eat or drink sth. 吃；喝
abundantly	/ə'bʌndəntli/	adv.	in large quantities 大量地
synthetic	/sɪn'θetɪk/	adj.	artificial; made by combining chemical substances rather than being produced naturally by plants or animals 人造的；（人工）合成的
culture	/'kʌltʃə(r)/	v.	to grow a group of cells or bacteria for medical or scientific study 培养；培植
ground beef			the beef that has been ground 碎牛肉；牛肉馅儿
patty	/'pæti/	n.	finely chopped meat, fish, etc. formed into a small round flat shape 碎肉饼；鱼肉饼
bland	/blænd/	adj.	not having a strong or interesting taste 清淡的；无滋味的
affordable	/ə'fɔːdəbl/	adj.	having enough money or time to be able to buy or to do sth. 付得起的；合理的
algae	/'ældʒiː/	n.	very simple plants with no real leaves, stems, or roots that grow in or near water, including seaweed 藻；海藻
biofuel	/'baɪəʊfjuːəl/	n.	a gas, liquid, or solid from natural sources such as plants that is used as a fuel 生物燃料
figure	/'fɪɡə(r)/	n.	a number representing a particular amount, especially one given in official information （统计）数字
aquaculture	/'ækwəkʌltʃə(r)/	n.	the growing of plants in water for food 水产养殖（业）
chow	/tʃaʊ/	n.	(slang) food （俚语）吃的东西
disease-resistant	/dɪziːz rɪ'zɪstənt/	adj.	抗病的
customize	/'kʌstəmaɪz/	v.	to make or change sth. to suit the needs of the owner 订制；订做
texture	/'tekstʃə(r)/	n.	the way food or drink tastes or feels in your mouth, for example whether it is rough, smooth, light, heavy, etc. 口感；质地

Food 3 UNIT

Note

Genetically modified (GM) food refers to the food whose genome has been altered to express desired traits. 转基因食品

Exercise

Listen to the news report and answer the following questions.

1. What have researchers been doing to try to feed 9 billion people by 2050?
2. What are the advantages of eating insects?
3. Why do food experts predict that algae farming could become the world's biggest crop industry?
4. Why is the year 2011 considered a milestone in farmed fish?
5. What will you be able to customize through 3D printed dishes?

Part E Projects

Choose one of the following projects, or design one of your own, concerning the theme of this unit. Finish the project by giving a presentation on it in class and chairing a discussion afterwards.

1. Choose a food-related item from China's Intangible Cultural Heritage List and research its origin, history, and current status. Create a video or presentation to share your findings with the class.
2. Search the Internet to identify countries or regions suffering from food shortages or insecurity. Explore the causes and propose some solutions.
3. Design a questionnaire to assess college students' awareness of and attitudes towards genetically modified food. Summarize your findings and present the results in class.

UNIT 4 Travel

Part A Spain's Tourist Hotspots Facing Housing Crisis

Vocabulary Preparation

hotspot	/ˈhɒtspɒt/	n.	a place where there is a lot of activity or entertainment 热点
soaring	/ˈsɔːrɪŋ/	adj.	increasing rapidly above the usual level 高耸的
steeply	/ˈstiːpli/	adv.	by a very large or sudden amount 突然地；急剧地
magnify	/ˈmæɡnɪfaɪ/	v.	to make sth. bigger, louder, or stronger 扩大；增强
influx	/ˈɪnflʌks/	v.	the fact of a lot of people, money, or things arriving somewhere 涌入；流入
magnet	/ˈmæɡnət/	n.	a person, place, or thing that sb./sth. is attracted to 磁体；有吸引力的人或事物
accommodation	/əˌkɒməˈdeɪʃn/	n.	somewhere to live or stay, often also providing food or other services 住宿；膳宿
kilter	/ˈkɪltə(r)/	n.	proper or usual state or condition 良好状态；平衡
out of kilter			not agreeing with or the same as sth. else 不匹配；不适合
speculative	/ˈspekjʊlətɪv/	adj.	(of business activity) done in the hope of making a profit but involving the risk of losing money 投机性的
high season			the time of year when a hotel or tourist area receives most visitors（旅馆或旅游地区的）旺季
sustain	/səˈsteɪn/	v.	to make sth. continue for some time without becoming less 使保持；使稳定持续

Notes

1. **Ibiza** is a Spanish island in the Mediterranean Sea off the eastern coast of the Iberian Peninsula. 西班牙伊维萨岛
2. **Balearic Islands** are an archipelago in the western Mediterranean Sea, near the

eastern coast of the Iberian Peninsula. The archipelago forms a province and autonomous community of Spain. 西班牙巴利阿里群岛

3. **Formentera** is a Spanish island located in the Mediterranean Sea, which belongs to the Balearic Islands autonomous community. 福门特拉岛（西班牙巴利阿里群岛的一部分）

4. **O Beach** is a renowned day club located on the west coast of Ibiza in San Antonio. The club is particularly famous for its elaborate events and eclectic music. O 海滩

Exercise 1

Listen to the news report and get the main idea.

What is the main idea of the news report?

A. Many workers in Ibiza are choosing to live in their cars due to the high cost of living.

B. Tourism has increased rental costs, causing a housing crisis for locals and businesses.

C. The local authorities in Ibiza are implementing new laws to control the housing market.

D. Ibiza's housing market is influenced by the influx of foreign visitors looking for short-term rentals.

Exercise 2

Listen to the news report again and fill in the blanks with the exact words or phrases.

Anchorwoman: Going next to the Spanish island of Ibiza and the 1. _____ cost of a place to live there. In many parts of Spain, rental costs have risen steeply in recent years. But in the tourist hotspot of Ibiza, the rise has been 2. _____ by the influx of foreign visitors. And that's left many locals unable to find affordable accommodation and businesses struggling to find vital staff. As Guy Hedgecoe reports.

Guy Hedgecoe: Ibiza is preparing for the summer tourist season. Its beaches and resorts have long been a(n) 3. _____ for holidaymakers, but its success has helped create a housing crisis. Across the Balearic Islands, rental costs have increased by nearly 20% over the last year alone, and in Ibiza, the increases

	have been even sharper. There are several reasons for the 4. _____ rise in rental costs. Higher interest rates and a higher cost of living have discouraged people from buying property. That, in turn, has led to an increase in demand for rented accommodation, pushing up rental rates.
Guy Hedgecoe:	Tourism is also a major factor. Last year, 3.7 million people visited Ibiza and the 5. _____ island of Formentera. Many stay in flats, pushing up rental prices and keeping locals out of the housing market. Cesar Nebrera is a chef, but although he has work, he's been sleeping in his car for the last three years, something which many workers on the island now resort to.
Cesar Nebrera:	Near Ibiza, accommodation is very expensive and it's getting more and more expensive. The cost of renting is completely 6. _____ with what you earn. When you've been living this long in a car, there comes a moment when you say, "I can't do this anymore. I need a home."
Guy Hedgecoe:	Local activists are demanding that this phenomenon be stopped.
Daniel Granda:	The problem we have is that the island's housing is not being used for the purpose for which it was built; it's being used as a(n) 7. _____ business and for tourism.
Guy Hedgecoe:	This situation is affecting local businesses. The O Beach disco and restaurant is preparing for the 8. _____, but finding staff in Ibiza or from elsewhere is not easy.
George McBlain:	I've already got friends on the island whose rent has doubled in the last year. So, when you are looking at workers coming to the island, it's a massive factor and it's well known. So, I think it will 9. _____ affect people coming to the island and getting workers to come to Ibiza.
Guy Hedgecoe:	The local authorities say the housing crisis is caused by homeowners who break the law by offering their properties to rent for short periods.
Juan Miguel Costa:	The problem is that you earn much more money renting for days or for weeks than if you rent according to the law,

	which is at least six months. We have a lot of people who is now renting illegally, offering their properties illegally.
Guy Hedgecoe:	As the high season approaches, the question is whether Ibiza's success as a tourism destination can be **10.** _____ when housing is such a problem. Guy Hedgecoe, BBC News, Ibiza.

Part B How "Trashy" Tourism Threatens World-Famous Destinations

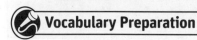

in its wake			as a result or consequences of it 随后；随之而来
pile-up	/ˈpaɪl ʌp/	n.	an accumulation of a specified thing 堆积；积聚
accessible	/əkˈsesəbl/	adj.	that can be reached, entered, used, seen, etc. 可到达的；可接近的；可进入的；可使用的
hop	/hɒp/	v.	to get on a plane, bus, etc. 登上（飞机、汽车等）
disposable	/dɪˈspəʊzəbl/	adj.	made to be thrown away after use 用后即丢弃的；一次性的
toss	/tɒs/	v.	to throw sth. lightly or carelessly（轻轻或漫不经心地）扔；抛；掷
landmark	/ˈlændmɑːk/	n.	sth., such as a large building, that you can see clearly from a distance and that will help you to know where you are 陆标；地标
circular	/ˈsɜːkjələ(r)/	adj.	moving around in a circle 环行的；绕圈的
tap	/tæp/	v.	to make use of a source of energy, knowledge, etc. that already exists 利用；开发；发掘
mindful	/ˈmaɪndfl/	adj.	remembering sb./sth. and considering them when you do sth. 记着；想着；考虑到

1. **Mount Qomolangma** is Earth's highest mountain above sea level, located in the Mahalangur Himal sub-range of the Himalayas. 珠穆朗玛峰

2. **Machu Picchu** is a 15th-century Inca citadel located in the Eastern Cordillera of southern Peru on a 2,430-meter mountain ridge. 秘鲁马丘比丘

3. **Stonehenge** is a prehistoric megalithic structure on Salisbury Plain in Wiltshire, England. 英国巨石阵

4. **Boracay** is a resort island in the Western Visayas region of the Philippines. 菲律宾长滩岛

Exercise

Listen to the news report and choose the best answer to each of the following questions.

1. How has the number of international tourist arrivals changed compared with 70 years ago?

   A. Decreased by 25 million.

   B. Increased by exactly 25 million.

   C. Increased to about 1.4 billion.

   D. Remained approximately the same.

2. What issue does Alton Byers focus on in the villages near Qomolangma?

   A. Reducing plastic use by tourists.

   B. Enhancing recycling facilities for tourists.

   C. Formulating waste management strategies.

   D. Implementing sustainable disposal methods for tourist waste.

3. Which of the following is NOT listed as a site struggling with trash issues according to the news report?

   A. Boracay.   B. Stonehenge.

   C. Mount Qomolangma.   D. The Eiffel Tower.

4. Why has the pile-up of trash been increasing at tourist sites?

   A. It is due to the impacts of natural disasters.

   B. It is because of local governmental neglect.

   C. It is due to tourism becoming more accessible.

   D. It is because of increased industrial activity nearby.

5. What solution do Byers and Beaudoin advocate for managing trash at tourist sites?

   A. Implementing stricter laws against littering.

   B. Banning plastic products at all tourist sites.

   C. Promoting mindfulness and global collective efforts.

   D. Introducing a tourist tax to fund clean-up operations.

Part C Rise of Adventure Tourism

Vocabulary Preparation

submersible	/səbˈmɜːsəbl/	n.	a submarine that goes underwater for short periods 可潜船；潜水器
lure	/lʊə(r)/	n.	the attractive qualities of sth. 吸引力；诱惑力
blast	/blɑːst/	v.	to leave the ground 发射升空
trek	/trek/	v.	to spend time walking, especially in mountains and for enjoyment and interest 远足；徒步旅行
moonshot	/ˈmuːnʃɒt/	n.	a plan or aim to do sth. that seems almost impossible 几乎不可能实现的任务
across the board			involving everyone or everything in a company, an industry, etc. 全体；整体
kayak	/ˈkaɪæk/	v.	a light canoe in which the part where you sit is covered over（坐的部分遮盖起来的）独木舟；单人划子；皮艇
zodiac	/ˈzəʊdiæk/	n.	the imaginary area in the sky in which the sun, moon, and planets appear to lie, and which has been divided into 12 equal parts each with a special name and symbol 黄道带；十二星座
gorilla	/gəˈrɪlə/	n.	a very large powerful African ape covered with black or brown hair 大猩猩
rogue	/rəʊg/	n.	a man who is dishonest and immoral 骗子；恶棍；流氓
scuba	/ˈskuːbə/	n.	an apparatus utilizing a portable supply of compressed gas (such as air) supplied at a regulated pressure and used for breathing while swimming underwater 水肺；便携式水下呼吸器
scuba diving			the sport of swimming underwater with special breathing equipment 戴水肺潜水
soul searching			deep and careful thought about your feelings, especially in relation to a moral problem or decision 自我反省
parasailing	/ˈpærəseɪlɪŋ/	n.	the sport of being pulled up into the air behind a boat while wearing a special parachute 帆伞运动；水上拖伞运动

Notes

1. **Titanic** is a British ocean liner that sank on 15 April, 1912 as a result of striking an iceberg on its maiden voyage from Southampton, England to New York City, the United States. 泰坦尼克号（英国 1912 年沉没的巨型邮轮）

2. **Rwanda** is a landlocked country in the Great Rift Valley of Central Africa.（非洲国家）卢旺达

3. **Silverbacks** are mature, adult male gorillas known for the distinctive patch of silver fur on their backs, which develops as they age. 银背大猩猩

4. **Bahamas** is an island country within the Lucayan Archipelago in the Atlantic Ocean. 巴哈马（位于大西洋西岸的一个岛国）

Exercise

Listen to the news report and decide whether the following statements are true (T) or false (F).

1. The lure of extreme adventure tourism often comes from the high risk associated with such activities. (   )
2. The global extreme adventure tourism industry is expected to exceed 10 billion dollars in 2023. (   )
3. Adventure tourists typically seek experiences where they can interact closely with wildlife in their natural habitats, as part of their travel. (   )
4. According to the news report, all incidents involving tourists in extreme conditions have been fatal. (   )
5. The existence of a company offering adventure tourism activities guarantees that the activities are safe. (   )

 Part D What Happens When You Use Your Mobile Phone in the Largest Resort in the World?

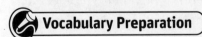

optimal	/ˈɒptɪməl/	*adj.*	best or most favorable 最佳的，最优的
throng	/θrɒŋ/	*n.*	a crowd of people 聚集的人群；一大群人

44

microcell	/ˌmaɪkrəʊˈsel/	n.	a device in a cellular network that is linked to a tower 微蜂窝；微基站
traffic	/ˈtræfɪk/	n.	the movement of messages and signals through an electronic communication system 信息流量；通信（量）
excruciatingly	/ɪkˈskruːʃieɪtɪŋli/	adv.	in a way that is extreme and difficult to bear 极端地；难以忍受地
livestream	/ˈlaɪvstriːm/	n.	a broadcast of the video and sound of an event over the Internet as it happens 直播（视频）
megabyte	/ˈmeɡəbaɪt/	n.	a unit of computer memory, equal to one million bytes 兆字节；百万字节
consistent	/kənˈsɪstənt/	adj.	in agreement with sth.; not contradicting sth. 与……一致的；相符的

 Notes

1. **Amusement park** is a large park which has a lot of things that you can ride and play on and many different activities to enjoy. 游乐场；娱乐园
2. **Universal Beijing Resort** is a theme park and entertainment resort complex based in Beijing, China. 北京环球度假区
3. **TikTok** is a social media platform for creating, sharing, and discovering short videos. 抖音短视频国际版 TikTok

Exercise

Listen to the news report and answer the following questions.

1. What is the size of the area within which the 4G and 5G networks can support phone users at Universal Beijing Resort?
2. What percentage of the 5G offload ratio has been reached according to the user traffic data mentioned in the news report?
3. What types of activities can visitors engage in while waiting in long queues, thanks to the 5G network?
4. How does the app enhance visitor experience in terms of wait time management at Universal Beijing Resort?
5. What is the significance of Universal Beijing Resort's role as a pilot platform for 5G infrastructure in the context of global tourism and technology?

Part E Projects

Choose one of the following projects, or design one of your own, concerning the theme of this unit. Finish the project by giving a presentation on it in class and chairing a discussion afterwards.

1. Research and present how technology is enhancing tourist experience at destinations throughout China. Focus on innovations such as virtual reality (VR) tours of historical sites like the Forbidden City, mobile apps offering navigation and cultural information for attractions like the Great Wall, and digital pass systems used in major amusement parks like Shanghai Disneyland. Evaluate the effectiveness of these technologies in improving visitor satisfaction and engagement. Additionally, propose further improvements or new technologies that could be introduced to enhance tourist experience in China.

2. Conduct a detailed study on the pioneering tourism practices being implemented across China, focusing specifically on eco-tourism initiatives and creative marketing strategies that promote lesser-known destinations. Explore examples such as the development of sustainable tourism in Yunnan's ancient towns, the promotion of rural tourism in regions like Guilin, and the use of digital media to attract visitors to remote yet culturally-rich areas like Gansu. Highlight how these innovations enhance both tourist satisfaction and the well-being of local communities.

3. Explore the modern revival of the Silk Road as a tourism route. Identify the key destinations along the route within China and examine how this historical trade route has been transformed into a cultural tourism pathway. Discuss the benefits this transformation has brought to regional development and international relations.

UNIT 5 Fashion

Part A Is Virtual Shopping the Future?

Vocabulary Preparation

photo-realistic	/ˈfəʊtəʊˌriːəˈlɪstɪk/	adj.	closely or accurately depicting that which is being copied or imitated 真实感的；逼真的
algorithm	/ˈælɡərɪðəm/	n.	a series of mathematical steps, especially in a computer program, which will give you the answer to a particular kind of problem or question（尤指电脑程序中的）算法；运算法则
nuance	/ˈnjuːɑːns/	n.	a subtle difference in meaning or opinion or attitude 细微差别
encapsulate	/ɪnˈkæpsjuleɪt/	v.	to represent all their most important aspects in a very small space or in a single object or event 概括；概述
immersive	/ɪˈmɜːsɪv/	adj.	used to describe a computer system or image that seems to surround the user（计算机系统或图像）沉浸式虚拟现实的
avatar	/ˈævətɑː(r)/	n.	a picture of a person or an animal which represents a person, on a computer screen, especially in a computer game or chat room 化身；头像

Notes

1. **Amazon's Echo Look** is a first of its kind echo focused on style, with Echo Look simply saying, "Alexa, take a photo" or "Alexa, take a video" to build your own personal lookbook, no smartphone camera or mirror required. 亚马逊 "私人搭配师"（内置语音助手 Alexa）

2. **E-commerce** is commerce conducted electronically (as on the Internet). 电子商务

3. **Holy Grail** is the bowl used by Jesus at the Last Supper. In the passage, it means something that people want and are looking for but that is extremely difficult to find or get. 圣杯（原指 "最后晚餐中耶稣使用的杯子"，在本语篇中是指 "人们一直寻找但很难找到或者得到的东西"）

Fashion 5 UNIT

Exercise 1

Listen to the news report and get the main idea.

What is the main point of the news report?

A. Advanced technologies are significantly transforming the way we shop for fashion.

B. Amazon's Echo Look aims to enhance the digital shopping experience by providing more interactive, immersive, and personalized options.

C. Some traditional roles may not be directly replaced by these advancements and are expected to evolve from the improved production and retail processes.

D. Creating a shopping experience that closely mimics real-world interactions is the goal.

Exercise 2

Listen to the news report again and fill in the blanks with the exact words or phrases.

Rachel: In the future, getting dressed may involve a lot more tech than you ever expected.

Hana Singh (Founder and CEO of OBSESS): So this is where, you know, you can see, like, it's really photo-realistic quality, even though it's 3D.

Rachel: I see the fur, like moving. First up, Amazon's Echo Look. They call it a(n) **1.** _____. So, we put it to the test, "Alexa, Alexa, Alexa, take a picture", against an actual stylist.

Man: I want to see. Oh, my gosh, that's crazy. And then there we go.

Rachel: Let's do a style check.

Rachel: Its **2.** _____ takes some time, but when it's done, it ranks which one it likes the best.

Rachel: According to Alexa, I am supposed to wear the light blue daytime outfit. Oh, they say the color is better for you. The outfit **3.** _____ works better for you.

Rachel: Amazon's algorithm doesn't stop at telling you what looks good. It also tries to sell you clothes, but its suggestions are hit or miss. And while the Echo Look may help you decide between two looks, it can't **4.** _____ the nuance of where you're going.

Rachel: But when you hear about the development of all these advanced technologies, do you worry about the future of your job?

Man:	For me, I personally don't. I think with, you know, the future of technology and fashion. I think it will benefit, like, production and retail. As a stylist, there's just that, you know, interpersonal 5. _____ that you can't replace.
Rachel:	Since the 6. _____ of e-commerce how we shop is moving away from stores. Some tech companies are trying to enhance the 7. _____ shopping experience by introducing AR and VR.
Rachel:	How do you see AR and VR changing the shopping experience?
Neha:	We see it changing completely. Like, if you think about e-commerce, every brand and every product essentially looks the same online. That doesn't encapsulate like what the brand is about. So, we are building the technology that will enable any brand and retailer to create amazing, 8. _____, discovery-based shopping experiences.
Rachel:	Is it really that much better than online shopping is currently?
Neha:	You have to try it. And with this technology, we are getting closer and closer to the real world, because the real world is three-dimensional. It's all around us. It's not just. So whatever technology, it can get us closer to the real world, like, that's going to be the next thing. Eventually this will be you, because that's the Holy Grail for fashion. It is like I want to see how I look in this. Not only do you need a 3D model, but you need the 9. _____ built into this model to see how this 10. _____ flows. Like, how it kind of stretches. Yeah. So, all of that like is going is becoming possible. We are not quite there yet.
Rachel:	If AR and VR want to change how we shop, digital avatars need to actually look and move like humans. Researchers from the Max Planck Institute for Intelligent Systems created cloth cap, which captures how clothing moves on a digital avatar. It can also estimate how clothing looks on different body types. It'll be years before we're shopping in our bedrooms in AR and VR, but technology is getting smarter, and so might our style.

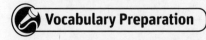

Part B   Style Meets Tech at Guangdong Fashion

Vocabulary Preparation

versatility	/ˌvɜːsəˈtɪləti/	n.	having a wide variety of skills 多才多艺；技术全面；用途广泛

thermal	/ˈθɜːməl/	adj.	caused by or designed to retain heat 保暖的
hemorrhoid	/ˈheməˌrɔɪd/	n.	pain caused by venous swelling at or inside the anal sphincter 痔疮
agile	/ˈædʒaɪl/	adj.	moving quickly and lightly 敏捷的；灵敏的
restock	/ˌriːˈstɒk/	v.	to stock again 补充；为（商店等）备办新货
patented	/ˈpeɪtəntɪd/	adj.	(of devices and processes) protected by patent 有专利权的
craftsmanship	/ˈkrɑːftsmənʃɪp/	n.	the level of skill shown by sb. in making sth. beautiful with his/her hands 技艺；手艺
heritage	/ˈherɪtɪdʒ/	n.	the history, traditions, and qualities that a country or society has had for many years and that are considered an important part of its character 遗产；传统
unveil	/ˌʌnˈveɪl/	v.	to show or introduce a new plan, product, etc. to the public for the first time 推出；揭幕
supply chain			the series of processes involved in the production and supply of goods, from when they are first made, grown, etc. until they are bought or used（产品）供应链
apparel	/əˈpærəl/	n.	clothing, when it is being sold in shops or stores（商店出售的）服装

Notes

1. **Influencer** is someone who is able to persuade a lot of people, for example, their followers on social media, to do, buy, or use the same things like they do. 网红

2. **Big data analysis** is the process of uncovering trends, patterns, and correlations in large amounts of raw data to help make data-informed decisions. 大数据分析

3. **Alibaba** focuses on online shopping, retail, the Internet, and technology. It helps people buy and sell things online through person-to-person, business-to-customer, and business-to-business sales. Alibaba owns and runs many companies worldwide in various industries. 阿里巴巴集团

4. **JD.com**, also known as Jingdong, formerly called 360 Buy, is a Chinese e-commerce company headquartered in Beijing. 京东商城

Exercise

Listen to the news report and choose the best answer to each of the following questions.

1. What is a key trend in this year's Runway highlights?

   A. Traditional fabric usage.

   B. Smart fabrics and AI production systems.

   C. Only focusing on men's clothing.

   D. Exclusively using recycled materials.

2. What challenge is China's apparel industry currently facing?

   A. Competition from Southeast Asia.

   B. Decreasing global demand.

   C. Lack of skilled workers.

   D. Environmental regulations.

3. What was prominent at the Guangdong Fashion Week?

   A. Only showcasing foreign brands.

   B. Combining high-tech fabrics with traditional designs.

   C. Focusing solely on digital fashion.

   D. Exclusively promoting sustainable practices.

4. What role do e-commerce giants like Alibaba and JD.com play in Guangdong Fashion Week?

   A. They provide traditional retail spaces.

   B. They bring the latest fashion directly to consumers.

   C. They focus on wholesale distribution.

   D. They organize the Runway shows.

5. What are considered main drivers for growth in China's retail apparel market?

   A. New fabrics, innovative designers, and international branding.

   B. Decreasing production costs and government subsidies.

   C. Relying on domestic sales, focusing on local markets, and promoting sustainable practices.

   D. The most complete supply chain, high-end customers, and traditional craftsmanship.

Unit 5 Fashion

Part C Why Milan Leads the Fashion Pack?

Vocabulary Preparation

columnist	/ˈkɒləmnɪst/	n.	a journalist who writes regular articles for a newspaper or magazine 专栏作家
eclipse	/ɪˈklɪps/	v.	to make sb./sth. seem dull or unimportant by comparison 使失色；使相形见绌
chandelier	/ˌʃændəˈlɪə(r)/	n.	a large round frame with branches that hold lights or candles 吊灯；枝形吊灯
tiara	/tiˈɑːrə/	n.	a piece of jewellery like a small crown decorated with precious stones, worn by a woman, for example a princess, on formal occasions 冠状头饰
angst	/æŋst/	n.	a feeling of anxiety and worry about a situation, or about your life 忧虑，焦虑
wrecked	/rekt/	adj.	completely destroyed or ruined 毁坏的；破裂的
palazzo	/pəˈlɑːtsəʊ/	n.	a large imposing building (such as a museum or a place of residence) especially in Italy 宫殿；邸宅
emanate	/ˈeməneɪt/	v.	to produce or show sth. 散发；产生；显示
dud	/dʌd/	n.	an event that fails badly or is totally ineffectual; a thing that is useless, especially because it does not work correctly 哑弹；不中用的东西
silhouette	/ˌsɪluˈet/	n.	the outline that it has, which often helps you to recognize it; the solid dark shape that you see when sb./sth. has a bright light or pale background behind them 轮廓；体形
selvage	/ˈselvɪdʒ/	n.	the edge of a fabric that is woven so that it will not ravel or fray; border consisting of an ornamental fringe at either end of an oriental carpet 布边；织边；镶边
gorgeous	/ˈɡɔːdʒəs/	adj.	very beautiful and attractive; giving pleasure and enjoyment 美丽动人的；令人愉快的

Notes

1. **WSJ (The Wall Street Journal)** is an American newspaper based in New York City, with a focus on business and finance.《华尔街日报》(美国纽约出版的报纸，以财经新闻报道为主）

2. **Gucci** was founded in 1921 by Guccio Gucci (1881–1953), which is an Italian luxury fashion house based in Florence, Italy. 古驰（全球奢侈品品牌之一）

3. **Swing from the chandeliers** is a way to describe a wild party where people do crazy, silly things and have a fun time. 尽情摇摆；举办疯狂的时尚派对

4. **Alessandro Michele** (1972–), the eccentric Italian designer who helped lift Gucci to a more than $10 billion brand, became Valentino's Creative Director in April 2024. 亚历山德罗·米歇尔（华伦天奴创意总监）

5. **Prada** is an Italian luxury fashion house founded in 1913 in Milan by Mario Prada. It specializes in leather handbags, travel accessories, shoes, ready-to-wear, and other fashion accessories.（意大利奢侈时尚品牌）普拉达

6. **Dolce and Gabbana**, also known by initials D&G, is an Italian luxury fashion house founded in 1985 in Legnano by Italian designers Domenico Dolce and Stefano Gabbana.（意大利奢侈时尚品牌）杜嘉班纳（也称为 D&G）

7. **Moschino** is an Italian luxury fashion house specializing in apparel, shoes, leather accessories, perfumes, and more.（意大利奢侈时尚品牌）莫斯奇诺

8. **Jeremy Scott** (1975–) is the sole owner of his namesake label, and from October 2013 to March 2023, was the creative director of the fashion house Moschino. 杰里米·斯科特（同名品牌的唯一拥有人）

9. **Marni Group S.r.l.**, commonly known as Marni, is an Italian luxury fashion house founded in 1994 by Consuelo Castiglioni in Milan, Italy.（意大利奢侈时尚品牌）玛尼

10. **Roberto Cavalli** (1940–2024) was an Italian fashion designer and inventor. He was known for exotic prints and for creating the sand-blasted look for jeans. The Roberto Cavalli fashion house sells luxury clothing, perfume, and leather accessories. 罗伯托·卡瓦利（意大利时装设计师和发明家）

11. **Peter Dundas** (1969–) is a Norwegian-American designer whose own label, Dundas, made its debut on Beyoncé at the 2017 Grammy Awards. 彼得·邓达斯（挪威裔美国设计师）

12. **Anna Cleveland** (1989–), a Dutch-born supermodel, is one of the most prominent faces in the fashion industry. 安娜·克利夫兰

13. **Jethro Tully** is a character from the comic series *The Walking Dead*. 杰思罗·塔利

Fashion 5 UNIT

Exercise

Listen to the news report and decide whether the following statements are true (T) or false (F).

1. Christina believes that Milan has always been the leading city in the fashion conversation. (　　)
2. Gucci is mentioned as a brand that is currently setting trends in Milan. (　　)
3. Prada's recent show was described as being a standout collection after a period of being sleepy. (　　)
4. Moschino's show by Jeremy Scott featured models with smoke machines under their gowns. (　　)
5. Marni's fall collection included heavy wool materials to prepare for the summer months. (　　)

Part D　Becoming Her Chinese Women's Fashion Evolution in the Past 70 Years

Vocabulary Preparation

puffy	/'pʌfi/	adj.	looking swollen; looking soft, round, and white 蓬松的；松软洁白的
frilled hem			a strip of fabric, lace, or ribbon tightly gathered or pleated on one edge and applied to a garment, bedding, or other textile as a form of trimming 大裙摆；有褶饰边裙脚
monotonous	/mə'nɒtənəs/	adj.	never changing and therefore boring 单调乏味的；毫无变化的
pervasiveness	/pə'veɪsɪvnəs/	n.	the quality of filling or spreading throughout 无处不在；普遍性

1. **Pager** is a small electronic device that you carry around with you and that shows a message or lets you know when somebody is trying to contact you, for example by making a sound. 传呼机；BP 机
2. **K-pop** is Korean pop music or fashion. 韩流（韩国潮流）；韩国流行音乐

Exercise

Listen to the news report and answer the following questions.

1. What were the features of the Blazy dress?
2. What was the only fashionable style in the 1960s?
3. What did career-minded women prefer in the 1980s?
4. What cultural influence led to a fashion boom in the 1990s?
5. What characterizes contemporary Chinese fashion?

Part E Projects

Choose one of the following projects, or design one of your own, concerning the theme of this unit. Finish the project by giving a presentation on it in class and chairing a discussion afterwards.

1. Clothing retailers like Zara, Forever 21, and H&M produce affordable, trendy clothing to meet the demands of young consumers. However, fast fashion has a significant environmental impact. According to the UN Environment Program, the fashion industry is the second-largest consumer of water and accounts for about 10% of global carbon emissions—more than all international flights and maritime shipping combined. Unfortunately, the problems associated with fast fashion are often overlooked by consumers. Discuss the environmental and social impacts of fast fashion, explore sustainable alternatives, and advocate for ethical practices within the industry.

2. Celebrities shape fashion trends through their public appearances, social media influence, and collaborations with fashion brands. Their style choices often set the tone for mainstream trends, inspiring fans across the globe. Suppose you are at a celebrity culture and media studies conference, presenting to media scholars and fashion marketers. You choose "The Influence of Celebrity Culture on Fashion Consumption" as your topic, analyzing how celebrity endorsements and personal styles impact consumer behavior.

3. Designers often incorporate vintage elements into their collections, blending nostalgic references with contemporary aesthetics to create fresh and innovative looks that resonate with today's fashion-conscious consumers. You are tasked with examining how past fashion eras influence modern styles, the role of nostalgia in trend cycles, and its significance in brand strategy. Additionally, discuss how nostalgia drives contemporary fashion trends in China.

UNIT 6 Lifestyle

Part A Lie down for a While at an Urban Oasis in Shanghai

Vocabulary Preparation

oasis	/əʊˈeɪsɪs/	n.	a calm, pleasant place in the middle of somewhere busy and unpleasant 绿洲；宁静宜人之地
slope	/sləʊp/	n.	a surface that lies at an angle to the horizontal so that some points on it are higher than others 斜坡
ergonomic	/ˌɜːgəˈnɒmɪk/	adj.	relating to the design of furniture or equipment which makes it comfortable and effective for people who use it 人体工程学的
scent	/sent/	n.	a pleasant natural smell 香味
plaza	/ˈplɑːzə/	n.	an open area or square in a town, especially in Spanish-speaking countries（尤指西班牙语国家城镇中的）露天广场
runway	/ˈrʌnweɪ/	n.	a long, level piece of ground with a specially prepared smooth, hard surface on which aircraft take off and land（飞机）跑道
density	/ˈdensəti/	n.	the number of people or things in a place when compared with the size of the place（人口等的）密度；稠密

Notes

1. **Xuhui Runway Park** is an innovative urban revitalization project that breathes new life into a unique piece of Shanghai's history. Located in the Xuhui Riverfront Area, a formal industrial zone of the city, this 14.63-hectare (36.15-acre) site was a runway for Longhua Airport. 上海徐汇跑道公园

2. **Longhua Airport** started off as an airfield in the 1920s. It is Shanghai's first civilian airport and remains in operation till now, albeit in a reduced capacity in its later days. 上海龙华机场

Exercise 1

Listen to the news report and get the main idea.

What is the main idea of the news report?

A. The importance of taking a 20-minute-break in the nature every day.

B. The design of a comfortable ergonomic slope.

C. The popularity of the Xuhui Runway Park as an urban oasis.

D. The renovation of Longhua Airport.

Exercise 2

Listen to the news report again and fill in the blanks with the exact words or phrases.

Zhang Hong: Here we are at the lunch break slope for office workers in Xuhui District. What makes it particularly popular is its ergonomic design, which makes it an ideal spot for a quick **1.** _____ . You might think I'm a bit crazy to be here at noon when it's already 26 degrees Celsius. But I heard it's so popular that finding a spot was almost impossible a few weeks ago. It's like lying down on a large deck chair with the pleasant scent of grass surrounding you. It's nice! The idea is known as the 20-minute **2.** _____ . Spending just 20 minutes in a natural setting can significantly **3.** _____ one's mind and body.

...

Zhang Hong: This public space has been around for about seven years. However, recent social media **4.** _____ have made it particularly popular among nearby office workers.

Zhang Dou: We are trying to build **5.** _____ down below so people around that can kind of look over to the activities in the sunken plaza. So, on the north side and the south side, we have benches. For this side, we decided to make it a little different, make it **6.** _____ . The angle is about 135 degrees—that's something we have tested many times in our office, trying to find a(n) **7.** _____ slope for people to lie down.

Zhang Hong: This slope is part of the Xuhui Runway Park. The over 14-hectare slide used to be a runway for Longhua Airport, which was Shanghai's only **8.** _____ airport until 1949.

Zhang Dou: Xuhui River from…It has a lot of high-density development. And I think they were smart when they were doing the master plan for this area. They have planned a riverfront **9.** _____ right along

Huangpu River. And then, when you go inside for a few blocks, they also planned this runway park, kind of in the middle of those high towers, so you can **10.** _____ from all those tall buildings.

Zhang Hong: Zhang Hong ICS from CGTN, Shanghai.

Part B Living off the Grid

Vocabulary Preparation

appeal	/əˈpiːl/	n.	a request to the public for money, information, or help（尤指向公众的）呼吁；求助；恳求
grid	/ɡrɪd/	n.	a system of wires through which electricity is connected to different power stations across a region 电力网；输电网
self-sufficient	/ˌself səˈfɪʃənt/	adj.	able to provide everything you need, especially food, for yourself without the help of other people（尤指食物）自给自足的
tremendously	/trɪˈmendəsli/	adv.	to a very great amount or level, or extremely well 巨大地；极好地
integrate	/ˈɪntɪɡreɪt/	v.	to mix with and join in society or a group of people, often changing to suit their way of life, habits, and customs（使）融入（某社会或群体）；（使）成为一体
sustainably	/səˈsteɪnəbli/	adv.	in a way that can continue over a period of time 持续地；能保持地；能维持地
drastic	/ˈdræstɪk/	adj.	(especially of actions) severe and sudden or having very noticeable effects 严厉的；猛烈的；激烈的
currently	/ˈkʌrəntli/	adv.	at the present time 目前；现在
sewage	/ˈsuːɪdʒ/	n.	waste matter such as water or human urine or solid waste 污水；污物
disposal	/dɪˈspəʊzl/	n.	the act of getting rid of sth., especially by throwing it away 清除；处理；抛弃
waste disposal			an electrical machine, connected to a kitchen sink, that cuts up food waste so that it will flow easily through the pipes 垃圾处理机

solar panel			a device that changes energy from the sun into electricity 太阳能电池板
hydroelectric	/ˌhaɪdrəʊɪˈlektrɪk/	adj.	producing electricity by the force of fast moving water such as rivers or waterfalls 水力发电的；水电的
turbine	/ˈtɜːbaɪn/	n.	a type of machine through which liquid or gas flows and turns a special wheel with blades in order to produce power 涡轮机；叶轮机；透平机
coppice	/ˈkɒpɪs/	n.	an area of closely planted trees in which the trees are cut back regularly to provide wood （尤指定期砍伐的）矮林；萌生林
hierarchical	/ˌhaɪəˈrɑːkɪkl/	adj.	arranged according to people's or things' level of importance, or relating to such a system 按等级划分的；等级制度的
consensus	/kənˈsensəs/	n.	a generally accepted opinion or decision among a group of people 一致的意见；共识
priority	/praɪˈɒrəti/	n.	sth. that is very important and must be dealt with before other things 优先考虑的事

 Notes

1. **Living off the grid** means not relying on public utilities for daily needs, instead using self-sufficient energy sources like solar, wind, and batteries, while managing waste independently. People adopt this lifestyle to reduce dependence on modern systems and pursue a more independent, eco-friendly, or simpler way of living. 离网生活

2. **The Back-to-the-Land Movement**, which emerged in the U.S. and U.K. in the 1940s, was driven by idealists seeking a simpler life. Its core goal was to create a better, more self-sufficient lifestyle away from society's dependence on materialism and fuel. "重返大地"运动

3. **Hippies** were part of a movement in the 1960s and 1970s that rejected mainstream American values. They developed a distinctive lifestyle, embraced communal living, adopted vegetarian diets focused on unprocessed foods, and practiced holistic medicine. 嬉皮士

Exercise

Listen to the news report and choose the best answer to each of the following questions.

1. How do Brithdir Mawr residents think of the modern way of living?

   A. They think it is much easier and simpler to live in the modern way.

   B. They disapprove of the modern way of living.

   C. They integrate modern ways of doing things into their lifestyle.

   D. They view it as a sustainable way to help the environment.

2. According to the news report, which of the following is NOT true about Brithdir Mawr?

   A. It has 23 residents now.

   B. The residents are in their mid-60s.

   C. It started in 1994.

   D. The residents live off the grid and in the community structure.

3. How is the intentional community developed?

   A. It develops from eco-villages and housing cooperatives.

   B. It can be traced back to the 1960s and 1970s.

   C. It's inspired by a movement in the 1940s.

   D. It's popularized by hippies in the U.S. and U.K.

4. How does Brithdir Mawr define the grid?

   A. It means electricity, water, and social network.

   B. It means electricity, food, and water.

   C. It means electricity, water, sewage, and waste disposal.

   D. It means food, water, heating, cooking, electricity, and milk.

5. What kind of community is Brithdir Mawr?

   A. It's a community charged by some members.

   B. It's a community valuing general agreement.

   C. It's a completely self-sufficient community.

   D. It's a quite challenging community.

Part C A Hygge Way to Happiness

Vocabulary Preparation

spike	/spaɪk/	n.	a sudden large increase in sth. 猛增；急升
shortlist	/'ʃɔːtlɪst/	v.	to judge the most suitable singular for a job or prize, made from a longer list of people originally considered 入围；提名
introvert	/'ɪntrəvɜːt/	n.	sb. who is shy and quiet, and prefers to spend time alone rather than often being with other people 性格内向者
indulgence	/ɪn'dʌldʒəns/	n.	an occasion when you allow sb. or yourself to have sth. enjoyable, especially more than is good for you 沉溺；放纵
Dane	/deɪn/	n.	a person from Denmark 丹麦人
inherently	/ɪn'hɪərəntli/	adv.	in a way that exists as a natural or basic part of sth. 内在地；本质上地
trendy	/'trendi/	adj.	modern and influenced by the most recent fashions or ideas 时髦的；受新潮思想影响的
catch-all	/'kætʃ ɔːl/	n.	a term or category which includes many different things 泛称，统称
ambiance	/'æmbɪəns/	n.	the character of a place or the quality it seems to have 气氛；情调；环境
per capita	/pə 'kæpɪtə/	adv.	amount for each person 人均（地）
savor	/'seɪvə(r)/	v.	to enjoy food or an experience slowly, in order to enjoy it as much as possible 细品；享用（食物）
sinful	/'sɪnfl/	adj.	against the rules of a religion or morally wrong 有罪过的；不道德的
life expectancy			the length of time that a living thing, especially a human being, is likely to live（尤指人的）预期寿命
zeitgeist	/'zaɪtɡaɪst/	v.	to become or possess the general set of ideas, beliefs, feelings, etc. that is typical of a particular period in history 成为时代思潮；具有时代精神

stateside	/'steɪtsaɪd/	adv.	related to the U.S.; in or towards the U.S. 在美国；往美国
impart	/ɪm'pɑːt/	v.	to communicate information to sb. 传授；告知
maternity leave			a period in which a woman is legally allowed to be absent from work in the weeks before and after she gives birth 产假
paternity leave			a period of time that a father is legally allowed to be away from his job so that he can spend time with his new baby 陪产假
monopoly	/mə'nɒpəli/	n.	complete control of sth., especially an area of business, so that others have no share 垄断；专卖；独占
groundedness	/'ɡraʊndɪdnɪs/	n.	the ability to make good decisions and not to say or do stupid things 明智；理智

Notes

1. **Instagram** is a social media platform that allows users to share photos and videos with their followers. 照片墙

2. **Pinterest** is a social site where you can collect and share images of the things you find interesting. You can also visually discover new interests by browsing the collections of other Pinterest users. 品趣志

3. **Scandinavia** is part of northern Europe, generally held to consist of the two countries of the Scandinavian Peninsula, Norway, and Sweden, with the addition of Denmark. 斯堪的纳维亚半岛（欧洲西北角半岛）

Exercise

Listen to the news report and decide whether the following statements are true (T) or false (F).

1. Hygge is a mixture of relaxation, indulgence, delicious food, gratitude, and equality. (   )

2. Danes don't always eat healthy food, but have less Type II diabetes. (   )

3. Denmark and the U.S. are among the top ten in the UN's World Happiness Report. (   )

4. Universal health care, equal gender opportunities, free university education,

and social security are some defining Danish features. (　)

5. When the Meyers have meals, they don't use the phones and often talk together. (　)

Part D　The Magic of Bookshops

Vocabulary Preparation

condense	/kənˈdens/	v.	to reduce sth., such as a speech or piece of writing, in length 压缩；缩短（讲话或文章）
roam	/rəʊm/	v.	to move about or travel, especially without a clear idea of what you are going to do 闲逛；漫步；漫游
anecdote	/ˈænɪkdəʊt/	n.	a short, often funny story, especially about sth. sb. has done 趣闻；轶事
meditation	/ˌmedɪˈteɪʃn/	n.	the act of giving your attention to only one thing, either as a religious activity or as a way of becoming calm and relaxed 默念；冥想
reiterate	/riˈɪtəreɪt/	v.	to say sth. again, once or several times 反复讲；重申
literati	/ˌlɪtəˈrɑːti/	n.	(*pl.*) people with a good education who know a lot about literature 文人；学士

Notes

1. **Jorge Carrión** (1976–) is a versatile writer, cultural critic, and director of the Master in Literary Creación at the Pompeu Fabra University. He is one of the most prominent writers of the Ibero-American generation born in the 1970s. 豪尔赫·卡里翁

2. **Kid's Republic** is a book haven for the children of Beijing. It opened in 2005 and was designed by Japanese architect Keiichiro Sako. It's stocked with picture books from all over the world and has an activity room that hosts storytelling events and anime screenings. It also offers one of the coolest settings for both kids and grown to interact with books. 蒲蒲兰绘本馆

3. **Page One**, a bookstore founded in Singapore in 1983, features rich and high-quality design and art books. It is a paradise for book lovers, especially for readers of design and art books, and children's literature. 叶一堂（书店）

Exercise

Listen to the news report and answer the following questions.

1. What is the book *Bookshop: A Reader's History* about?
2. How does Jorge Carrion keep a record of the bookstores he's visited?
3. What are Jorge Carrion's suggestions for Chinese bookshops?
4. How does Jorge Carrion think of Kid's Republic?
5. What's special about Page One?

Part E Projects

Choose one of the following projects, or design one of your own, concerning the theme of this unit. Finish the project by giving a presentation on it in class and chairing a discussion afterwards.

1. Investigate how satisfied urban residents are with their local parks. Prepare a list of interview questions to assess people's satisfaction with local parks in terms of accessibility, ecological quality, and diversity. Visit a nearby park in your neighborhood and interview at least five groups of people. Collect and analyze their feedback, and then present your findings to the class.

2. Keeping a mood journal is an example of self-monitoring, useful for gaining awareness and insight into one's own patterns and habits. For one week, keep a mood journal, recording the happy moments in your life during this time. Describe these moments in detail, including what happened, who was involved, when and where it occurred, and how it made you feel. Share your hygge approach to happiness with your classmates.

3. Visit some bookshops in your city and talk with the shop owners, staff, or readers if possible. Identify the unique features of each bookshop and take photos of its most captivating aspects. Create a video of your visits in English and share it with your classmates.

UNIT 7 Sports

Part A Health Benefits of Exercising Outdoors

Vocabulary Preparation

routine	/ruːˈtiːn/	n.	the normal order and way in which you regularly do things 常规；正常顺序
trump	/trʌmp/	v.	to beat sth. that sb. says or does by saying or doing sth. even better 赢；胜过；打败
caveat	/ˈkæviæt/	n.	a warning that particular things need to be considered before sth. can be done 警告；告诫
pound the pavement			to walk on a lot of city streets to get sth. done 走街串巷（尤指为了找工作或推销产品）；用力行走（为了锻炼身体）
strenuous	/ˈstrenjuəs/	adj.	needing great effort and energy 费力的；繁重的；艰苦的
workout	/ˈwɜːkaʊt/	n.	a period of physical exercise that you do to keep fit 锻炼；训练

 Note

The Washington Post is a morning daily newspaper published in Washington, D.C., the dominant newspaper in the U.S. capital and usually counted as one of the greatest newspapers in the U.S.《华盛顿邮报》

Exercise 1

Listen to the news report and get the main idea.

What's the main point of the news report?

A. Doing exercise indoors and outdoors have different benefits.

B. Doing exercise outdoors is far more beneficial than indoors.

C. Spring is the best time for people to do exercise outdoors.

D. People who live or work in big cities can exercise in city-urban areas.

Sports UNIT 7

Exercise 2

Listen to the news report again and fill in the blanks with the exact words or phrases.

Lara: All right, turning now to the warmer weather. We are looking at why taking your fitness routine outside might be more beneficial than working out indoors. It's a story we first saw in *The Washington Post*. Rhiannon Ally is in Central Park doing just that. Good morning to you, Rhiannon.

Rhiannon Ally: Hey, good morning, Lara. Yes, it is a(n) 1. _____ morning here in New York City. And millions of Americans, spring is finally showing its face everywhere you look. It is so beautiful out here. And we're talking green exercise this morning. And green exercise means exactly what you think. It's taking your exercise routine and 2. _____ into nature. And a review of 10 different studies looking at about 300 people found that there are big benefits. We're talking mental and physical benefits. It can help with your 3. _____. It can help with your willingness to stick to a routine. It can also just help you to work out even harder. In fact, in all of these studies of all the things they measured, indoor exercise did not 4. _____ outdoor exercise in any of the areas, Lara. So, it seems the research is pretty clear on this.

Lara: I mean, looking at you makes me want to just get out there and do it. I can see how it would work. But what do researchers think it is?

Rhiannon Ally: So, we've all heard the saying, I'm gonna go take a walk and clear my head or perhaps a lot of us have even said that ourselves. It 5. _____, there is something to that. When you get out into nature, it really forces you to put your worries aside, at least for the time being, to stop stressing so much, to really reset your brain. And that means afterwards, you can 6. _____ better. You can just do all things better than you could before that. And that's on top of the benefits we already know about, Lara. We're talking increased blood flow to and oxygen to your brain.

Lara: All right, but there are some 7. _____. It's not just as simple as getting out there, right?

Rhiannon Ally: So, there's always an exception, right? This is mainly for people who live or work in big cities or spend a lot of time there. We love looking at those big skyscrapers. They're beautiful. But when you're talking about 8. _____ the pavement, if you want those mental health benefits, you're not gonna get the same benefits if you're running in a city-urban area versus if you get out into a forest or a park, or even a beach. Just 9. _____ yourself in mother nature is where you're really gonna get those benefits. But you don't have to start out with these long, 10. _____ workouts. You want to work your way up to that. So, you want to talk to your doctor or perhaps your personal trainer. Set some small goals and then work your way up to that. And Lara, I know how much you love tennis. So I'm hoping today you can get out on the tennis court and play a game. I'm gonna go get my kids. We're gonna go for a walk in the park. I can't wait. Spring is finally here.

Lara: Oh, you got that right. I will be on the court. And I cannot wait to get out there. I'm so glad the weather is finally cooperating. And hey, great workout for the cameraman, too. Give him a good job. Everybody getting their outdoor, green workout on.

Part B Five-Year Runner on How the Sport Transformed His Life

Vocabulary Preparation

straight	/streɪt/	adv.	continuously without interruption 连续不断地
ultra	/ˈʌltrə/	adj.	doing beyond others or beyond due limit 超级的；极端的
byproduct	/ˈbaɪˌprɒdʌkt/	n.	sth. that is produced during the manufacture or processing of another product 副产品
mess up			to cause sth. to fail or be spoiled 把……搞糟；把……弄乱
phobia	/ˈfəʊbiə/	n.	a very strong irrational fear or hatred of sth. 恐惧症

intimidating	/ɪnˈtɪmɪdeɪtɪŋ/	adj.	frightening in a way which makes a person feel less confident 吓人的；令人胆怯的
subside	/səbˈsaɪd/	v.	to become calmer or quieter 趋于平静；平息；减弱；消退
invincible	/ɪnˈvɪnsəbl/	adj.	too strong to be defeated or changed 不可战胜的；不能改变的
receipt	/rɪˈsiːt/	n.	a piece of paper which shows that goods or services have been paid for 收据；收条

 Notes

1. **L.A.** short for Los Angeles, officially the City of Los Angeles, is a major city in California's southern California region. With a population of 3,792,621 as of 2010, Los Angeles is the second-largest city in the United States, after New York City, and the most populous city in California. 洛杉矶（美国第二大城市）

2. **Mali**, officially the Republic of Mali, is a landlocked country in West Africa. Mali is the eighth largest country in Africa. 马里（西非国家）

3. **Seattle** is a coastal seaport city and the seat of King County, in the U.S. state of Washington. Seattle is the largest city in both the State of Washington and the Pacific Northwest region of North America. 西雅图（美国一港市）

4. **Kelly Clarkson** (1982–) is an American singer and songwriter. In 2002, she rose to fame after winning the first season of *American Idol*, and has since been established as "The Original American Idol". 凯莉·克拉克森（美国知名女歌手、词曲创作人和演员）

5. **New York City Marathon** is an annual marathon (42.195 kilometers or 26.219 miles) that courses through the five boroughs of New York City. The race is organized by New York Road Runners and has been run every year since 1970. 纽约马拉松

Exercise

Listen to the news report and choose the best answer to each of the following questions.

1. Why did Hellah Sidibe start running as a routine?

   A. He started running to strengthen his body.

   B. He wanted to run faster because he is a soccer player.

   C. He wanted to overcome his fear of running.

D. He was punished by his soccer coach to run.

2. What do we know about Hellah's experience of running across America?

   A. He started from New York and ended in L.A.

   B. He ran through 14 states with 3,061 kilometers.

   C. He spent 84 days to run through L.A. and New York.

   D. He had to run 36 miles a day to fulfill the plan.

3. How did running end up saving Hellah?

   A. It helped him to become a soccer player.

   B. It helped him to find joy and hope in life again.

   C. It helped him to be a top soccer player in the world.

   D. It helped him to put his mind to soccer.

4. What did Hellah's wife do when he started running?

   A. She told him to be a YouTuber instead of a runner.

   B. She did the recording when he was running.

   C. She suggested him uploading his experience to YouTube.

   D. She introduced him to the public through YouTube.

5. What does Hellah think is important to be a runner?

   A. A runner has to run as fast as possible.

   B. A runner has to run as long as possible.

   C. A runner needs to walk for some distance after running.

   D. A runner needs persistence more than time.

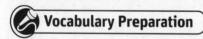

Part C   VR Sports

 Vocabulary Preparation

analog	/ˈænəlɒg/	adj.	(also *analogue*) using a continuously changing range of physical quantities to measure or store data 模拟的
augmented	/ɔːgˈmentɪd/	adj.	having been made greater in size or value 扩大的；增强的

72　新闻英语视听说（第五版）

overlay	/ˌəʊvəˈleɪ/	n.	a thing that is laid on top of or covers sth. else 覆盖物；涂层
disoriented	/dɪsˈɔːriəntɪd/	adj.	having lost one's bearings; confused as to time or place or personal identity 分不清方向或目标的；无判断力的
unplug	/ˌʌnˈplʌg/	v.	to disconnect (an electrical device) by removing its plug from a socket 拔去（电源）插头
panoramic	/ˌpænəˈræmɪk/	adj.	presenting a view of a wide area or all the different aspects of a particular subject, event, etc. 全景的；远景的；全貌的
tune	/tjuːn/	v.	to prepare or adjust sth. so that it is suitable for a particular situation 调整；使协调；使适合
entrepreneur	/ˌɒntrəprəˈnɜː(r)/	n.	a person who makes money by starting or running businesses, especially when this involves taking financial risks 创业者；企业家
flashy	/ˈflæʃi/	adj.	intended to impress by looking very skilful 炫耀技艺的；浮华的
resistance	/rɪˈzɪstəns/	n.	a force that stops sth. moving or makes it move more slowly 阻力；抗力
epic	/ˈepɪk/	adj.	very great and impressive 宏大的；壮丽的；给人深刻印象的
arena	/əˈriːnə/	n.	an area of activity that concerns the public, especially one where there is a lot of opposition between different groups or countries 斗争场所；竞争舞台；活动场所
compound	/ˈkɒmpaʊnd/	adj.	formed of two or more parts 复合的；组合的
beam	/biːm/	n.	a line of light, electric waves or particles 光线；（波）束
shard	/ʃɑːd/	n.	a piece of broken glass, metal, etc. 碎片
gamification	/ˌgeɪmɪfɪˈkeɪʃn/	n.	the process of adding games or game-like elements to sth. (as a task) so as to encourage participation 游戏化
dilation	/daɪˈleɪʃn/	n.	becoming or making sth. larger, wider, or more open 扩大；膨胀；扩张

Notes

1. **Black Box VR** was founded by fitness fanatics Ryan DeLuca & Preston Lewis in 2016, which combines VR with resistance training, gaming principles, and high intensity cardio for people trying to reach their health and fitness goals. 黑匣子虚拟现实健身房

2. **Ski Tech** is an indoor snow sports training center in Hong Kong, China with SkyTech VR technologies approved by U.S. Olympic Ski and Snowboard Team. 香港室内滑雪训练基地

Exercise

Listen to the news report and decide whether the following statements are true (T) or false (F).

1. Cyber sickness happens when people surf on the Internet for too long time. (　　)
2. At Ski Tech, people can experience what skiing is really like with man-made snow. (　　)
3. Doing sports at Black Box VR is gamified so as to make it easy for its members. (　　)
4. Black Box VR expects to make use of technology to help people stick to their fitness routine. (　　)
5. People doing sports at Black Box VR feel that time is passing much more slowly. (　　)

Part D Dragon Boat Festival—A Blend of Tradition and Competition

Vocabulary Preparation

rhythmic	/ˈrɪðmɪk/	adj.	having a regular pattern of sounds, movements, or events 有节奏（或规律）的；节奏分明的
flock	/flɒk/	v.	to go or gather together somewhere in large numbers 群集，聚集；蜂拥
pungent	/ˈpʌndʒənt/	adj.	having a strong taste or smell 味道（或气味）强烈的；刺激性的

pouch	/paʊtʃ/	n.	a small bag, usually made of leather, and often carried in a pocket or attached to a belt 小袋子；荷包
wormwood	/'wɜːmwʊd/	n.	a plant with a bitter flavor, used in making alcoholic drinks and medicines 蒿；苦艾
calamus	/'kæləməs/	n.	any tropical Asian palm of the genus calamus, some species of which are a source of rattan and canes 菖蒲
mint	/mɪnt/	n.	a plant with dark green leaves that have a fresh smell and taste and are added to food and drinks to give flavor, and used in cooking as a herb and to decorate food 薄荷
repel	/rɪ'pel/	v.	to drive, push, or keep sth. away 推开；赶走；驱除
ailment	/'eɪlmənt/	n.	an illness that is not very serious 轻病；小恙
dampness	/'dæmpnəs/	n.	moisture in the air, or on the surface of sth. 潮气；湿气
turn the tide			to cause a complete reversal of the circumstances 扭转局势；力挽狂澜

 Notes

1. **Dragon Boat Festival**, also commonly known as the Duanwu Festival, is a traditional and statutory holiday originating in China. The festival now occurs on the fifth day of the fifth month of the traditional lunar calendar. 端午节

2. **Qu Yuan** (340 B.C.–278 B.C.) is a Chinese poet who lived during the Warring States Period of ancient China. He is known for his contributions to classical poetry, especially through the poems of the Chu Ci anthology. 屈原

3. **Chinese Calendar** is a lunisolar calendar, incorporating elements of a lunar calendar with those of a solar calendar. It is not exclusive to China and is followed by many other Asian cultures as well. 农历；阴历

Exercise

Listen to the news report and answer the following questions.

1. What is the history of the Dragon Boat Festival, and what did people traditionally do to celebrate it?

2. In Chinese medicine, what is the relationship between nature and human body, and how do people fight against the threats to human body caused by the weather?

3. What is the weather like in many regions of China during the Dragon Boat Festival?

4. What are the herbs that people usually use to cure some illnesses during the Dragon Boat Festival?

5. What do paddlers who join in dragon boat races usually do before the competition and why?

Part E Projects

Choose one of the following projects, or design one of your own, concerning the theme of this unit. Finish the project by giving a presentation on it in class and chairing a discussion afterwards.

1. Conduct online research or a survey to learn about the health conditions of citizens in China, and assess their awareness of the importance of exercise and fitness. Present your findings to the class.

2. Search the Internet for successful athletes in any sport, and identify the qualities that have contributed to their success. Present your findings to the class.

3. Work in groups to gather some news reports on how sports have helped promote Chinese culture or contributed to the development of other industries, such as tourism or economy. Share your findings with your classmates and discuss the lessons we can learn from them.

UNIT 8 Entertainment

Part A Wordle—The Daily Obsession of Millions

Vocabulary Preparation

brainchild	/'breɪntʃaɪld/	n.	an idea or invention of one person or a small group of people（个人或小群体的）主意；发明
acquire	/ə'kwaɪə(r)/	v.	to obtain sth. by buying or being given it 购得；获得，得到
compelling	/kəm'pelɪŋ/	adj.	that makes you pay attention to it because it is so interesting and exciting 引人入胜的；扣人心弦的
foolproof	/'fuːlpruːf/	adj.	very well designed and easy to use so that it cannot fail and you cannot use it wrongly 使用简便的；完全可靠的；万无一失的
vowel	/'vaʊəl/	n.	a speech sound in which the mouth is open and the tongue is not touching the top of the mouth, the teeth, etc. 元音
blow	/bləʊ/	v.	to waste an opportunity 浪费（机会）；断送；搞砸
eliminate	/ɪ'lɪmɪneɪt/	v.	to remove or get rid of sb./sth. 排除；清除；消除

Notes

1. **Wordle** is a simple word game, in which the task is to guess a five-letter word. You have six tries. After each guess, the tiles change colors to show which letters are not in the word (gray), which letters are in the word but in the wrong position (yellow), and which ones are correctly in the word and in the right position (green). 一款猜词游戏

2. **The New York Times** is a morning daily newspaper published in New York City. It has long been the newspaper of record in the United States and is one of the world's great newspapers. Its strength lies in its editorial excellence.《纽约时报》

Exercise 1

Listen to the news report and get the main idea.

What is the main point of the news report?

A. Wordle is a really tricky and time-consuming game.

B. Wordle is developed with the joint efforts of editors.

Entertainment 8

C. Wordle has become the most popular game in the United States.

D. Wordle was astonishingly successful in 2022.

Exercise 2

Listen to the news report again and fill in the blanks with the exact words or phrases.

Anchor: Throughout the morning, our Susan Spencer is all about fun and games. First up, word play. For millions of Americans, morning means breakfast, coffee and—most importantly—Wordle.

Susan Spencer: I mean, my Wordle is usually done in the first 10 minutes of 1. _____.

Everdeen Mason: Yeah, I mean, some people, they play our puzzles the minute they come out.

Susan Spencer: Everdeen Mason is the editorial director of *The New York Times'* Games.

Zoe Bell: This has a good amount of space, though, in between.

Susan Spencer: Zoe Bell is its 2. _____. What do people think when you tell them what you do for a living?

Zoe Bell: It is a cocktail party winner.

Susan Spencer: Wordle, the brainchild of software engineer Josh Wardle, was 3. _____ by *The New York Times* in 2022. A year later, it was played 4.8 billion times.

Zoe Bell: Tens of millions of people are playing it every day.

Susan Spencer: OK, let's see what happens. Absolutely nothing, that's the worst possible result. If you're 4. _____ the game, here's how it works: Each day, there's a five-letter mystery word. You get six chances to figure it out. With each guess, you'll learn if your letters are wrong, right, or right but in the 5. _____. Can you put your finger on what it is in the design of Wordle that accounts for this astonishing success?

Zoe Bell: If you think about what happens with every guess in Wordle is you get new information and I think that's really compelling. And then when you solve it, there's a really, really big moment of 6. _____.

Susan Spencer:	Tell me about it. [Laughs] Well, it depends on how soon you solve it.
Everdeen Mason:	It might be a lot of other things too, or is it a better strategy to...
Susan Spencer:	OK, so what's the 7. _____ strategy for doing that?
Everdeen Mason:	You know, some people have the same word every single day.
Susan Spencer:	Is that a good idea?
Everdeen Mason:	It can be, I mean, especially if you pick one with a lot of vowels.
Susan Spencer:	ADIEU is the most popular first guess—all those vowels—but here's depressing news: Statistically, ADIEU does not 8. _____ the best results.
Zoe Bell:	I actually think that the starting word is important, but so is the second word. Because if you have a good starting word and then you blow it by not 9. _____ other letters in your second guess, then you're gonna be at five or six (tries).
Susan Spencer:	But this is the genius of its design.
Zoe Bell:	Right, yes.
Susan Spencer:	A genius that's made Wordle a national 10. _____ —"All we have is one lousy T." —at breakfast tables everywhere.

Part B Conservation Group Fighting to Save Marilyn Monroe's Los Angeles Home

Vocabulary Preparation

iconic	/aɪˈkɒnɪk/	adj.	important, impressive, acting as a sign or symbol of sth. 符号的；图标的；偶像的
drama	/ˈdrɑːmə/	n.	a real situation which is exciting or distressing; an exciting event 戏剧性事件；戏剧性情节；戏剧性场面
gem	/dʒem/	n.	a person, place, or thing that is especially good 难能可贵的人；风景优美的地方；美妙绝伦的事物
bungalow	/ˈbʌŋɡələʊ/	n.	a house built all on one level, without stairs 平房

Entertainment UNIT 8

spotlight	/'spɒtlaɪt/	n.	attention from newspapers, television, and the public 媒体和公众的注意；焦点
raze	/reɪz/	v.	to completely destroy a building, town, etc. so that nothing is left 彻底摧毁；将……夷为平地
nuisance	/'njuːsns/	n.	a thing, person, or situation that is annoying or causes trouble or problems 麻烦事；讨厌的人（或东西）
relish	/'relɪʃ/	v.	to get great pleasure from sth.; to want very much to do or have sth. 享受；渴望；喜欢

 Notes

1. **Marilyn Monroe** (1926–1962) was an American actress who became a major sex symbol, starring in a number of commercially successful films during the 1950s, and is considered a pop culture icon. 玛丽莲·梦露

2. *Gentlemen Prefer Blondes* is a 1953 American musical comedy film directed by Howard Hawks and written by Charles Lederer. 电影《绅士爱美人》

3. **Brentwood** is located in the heart of Northern California's Contra Costa County. Brentwood shines as a hidden gem, offering a blend of rural charm and modern convenience. Known for its scenic beauty, agricultural heritage, and welcoming atmosphere, Brentwood is a city that embodies the Central Valley lifestyle. 加利福尼亚州布伦特伍德

4. **Chinese Theater** is a Hollywood landmark known for hosting numerous movie premieres, the Academy Awards, and other events. It features the largest IMAX auditorium in the world and the third largest movie screen in North America. TCL 中国剧院

5. **Hollywood Walk of Fame** is the famous stretch of sidewalk along Hollywood Boulevard symbolizing glamour with the names of the most successful actors, filmmakers, musicians, and celebrities in history. 好莱坞星光大道

6. **Los Angeles Conservancy** is a non-profit membership organization whose mission is to work through education and advocacy to recognize, preserve, and revitalize the historic architectural and cultural resources of Los Angeles County. 洛杉矶文物保护协会

7. **Angels Flight Railway** is the world's shortest railway, offering a scenic ride between Hill Street and Grand Avenue on Bunker Hill. 天使飞行铁路

8. **Hollywood's Cinerama Dome** is a theater debuted in 1963 on Sunset Boulevard, which is known for its space-age looking dome and its wide, curved screen. 好莱坞圆顶剧院

Exercise

Listen to the news report and choose the best answer to each of the following questions.

1. What is Jeff Zarrinnam's mission?

    A. To protect L.A.'s landmarks.

    B. To link Marilyn Monroe's legacy with the public.

    C. To find Hollywood's hidden gems.

    D. To preserve the Hollywood sign.

2. What has happened over the 60 years after Marilyn Monroe died?

    A. The house was inherited by her family.

    B. The house was purchased and sold many times.

    C. The present owner wants to relocate it.

    D. The house was torn down long ago.

3. Which organization works to preserve culturally significant buildings?

    A. Angels Flight Railway.

    B. Los Angeles Conservancy.

    C. Cinerama Dome Theater.

    D. The Star Line.

4. According to Jeff Zarrinnam, what is the best solution for preserving Marilyn Monroe's home?

    A. To see her home from the street.

    B. To make a bus stop for her home.

    C. To find a better place for her home.

    D. To make it a recognizable piece of real estate

5. What has the city of L.A. done to honor the iconic Pink's?

    A. The city has relocated the famous building.

    B. The city has called for fans to come and enjoy the food.

    C. The city has renamed the intersection after the restaurant.

    D. It is unclear what the city has done so far.

Unit 8 Entertainment

Part C Pop-up Exhibition in Hong Kong Marks 50 Years of Bruce Lee's Death

Vocabulary Preparation

span	/spæn/	v.	to last all through a period of time or to cover the whole of it 持续；贯穿
premiere	/ˈpremieə(r)/	n.	the first public performance of a film/movie or play（电影、戏剧的）首次公演；首映
replica	/ˈreplɪkə/	n.	a very good or exact copy of sth. 复制品；仿制品
mural	/ˈmjʊərəl/	n.	a painting, usually a large one, done on a wall, sometimes on an outside wall of a building 壁画
fencing	/ˈfensɪŋ/	n.	the sport of fighting with long thin swords 击剑运动
incorporate	/ɪnˈkɔːpəreɪt/	v.	to include sth. so that it forms a part of sth. 将……包括在内；包含；吸收
mark	/mɑːk/	v.	to celebrate or officially remember an event that you consider to be important 纪念；庆贺
screening	/ˈskriːnɪŋ/	n.	the act of showing a film/movie or television program 放映；播放
debut	/ˈdeɪbjuː/	n.	the first public appearance of a performer or sports player 首次亮相；初次登台（或上场）
tailor-made	/ˌteɪləˈmeɪd/	adj.	made for a particular person or purpose, and therefore very suitable 特制的；专门设置的；非常合适的
rein	/reɪn/	n.	a long narrow leather band that is fastened around a horse's neck and is held by the rider in order to control the horse 缰绳
cater to			to provide the things that a particular person or situation needs or wants 满足需要；适合；迎合
snapshot	/ˈsnæpʃɒt/	n.	a short description or a small amount of information that gives you an idea of what sth. is like 简介；简要说明
signature	/ˈsɪɡnətʃə(r)/	n.	a particular quality that makes sth. different from other similar things and makes it easy to recognize 签名；明显特征；识别标志

Notes

1. **Jeet Kune Do** is a modern martial art incorporating elements of kungfu, fencing, and boxing, devised by the American actor Bruce Lee. 截拳道

2. *The Way of the Dragon* is a 1972 China Hong Kong action movie starring Bruce Lee. In the movie, a martial arts master visits his relatives at their restaurant in Italy and ends up defending them against brutal gangsters. 电影《猛龙过江》

3. *The Game of Death* is a 1972 film starring Bruce Lee. It was almost the film Bruce Lee had planned to be the demonstration piece of his martial art Jeet Kune Do. 电影《死亡游戏》

4. *Kill Bill* is the story of one retired assassin's revenge against a man who tried to kill her while she was pregnant years prior. After being in a coma for four years, Beatrix Kiddo is hungry for revenge against the man and his team of assassins and will stop at nothing to kill Bill. 电影《杀死比尔》

5. **Wing Chun** is a traditional Chinese martial art which is derived from kungfu. At its heart, it's known for its practicality, efficiency of movement, and its effectiveness in close-range combat. 咏春拳

6. *The Kid* is a drama film starring the then 10-year old Bruce Lee in his first leading role in the title role of "Kid Cheung", based on a comic book character written by Yuen Po Wan. 电影《细路祥》

7. **Fung Fung** (1920–2000) was an actor and director, known for *My Darling Grandchild* (1964), *Yue Guang Guang* (1965), and *Zhen Jia Qiao Lang Jun* (1957). 冯峰（中国粤剧男演员、导演）

8. **Tae Kwon Do** is a Korean martial art that translates the art of fist and foot. 跆拳道

9. **Karate** is a Japanese sport or way of fighting in which people fight using their hands, elbows, feet, and legs. 空手道

Exercise

Listen to the news report and decide whether the following statements are true or false.

1. Jeet Kune Do was founded by Bruce Lee without combining elements of other combat disciplines. (   )
2. In the pop-up display, visitors can read Bruce Lee's quotations. (   )
3. Many video games are influenced by *The Game of Death*. (   )
4. Bruce Lee acted in a film with the help of his father when he was nine years old. (   )
5. Director Fung Fung's daughter worked together with Bruce Lee in a film. (   )

Entertainment UNIT 8

 Part D Will Unique Popcorn Buckets Bring People Back into Movie Theaters?

Vocabulary Preparation

make waves			to be very active in a way that makes people notice you, and that may sometimes cause problems 咋咋呼呼；大肆张扬
meltdown	/'meltdaʊn/	n.	a complete failure, especially in financial matters 灾难；市场崩溃
tease	/ti:z/	v.	to laugh at sb. and make jokes about him/her, either in a friendly way or in order to annoy or embarrass him/her 取笑；戏弄；揶揄；寻开心
streaming	/'stri:mɪŋ/	n.	a method of transmitting data from the Internet directly to a user's computer screen without the need to download it 串流（传播）
recline	/rɪ'klaɪn/	v.	to sit or lie in a relaxed way, with your body leaning backwards 斜倚；斜躺；向后倚靠
entice	/ɪn'taɪs/	v.	to persuade sb./sth. to go somewhere or to do sth., usually by offering them sth. 诱使；引诱
collectible	/kə'lektəbl/	adj.	being worth collecting (not necessarily valuable or antique) 有收藏价值的
concession	/kən'seʃn/	n.	the right to sell sth. in a particular place; the place where you sell it, sometimes an area which is part of a larger building or store 特许经营权；销售场地；摊位
vessel	/'vesl/	n.	a container used for holding liquids, such as a bowl, cup, etc. 容器；器皿
release	/rɪ'li:s/	n.	the act of making sth. available to the public 发行；发布
viral	/'vaɪrəl/	adj.	used to describe sth. that quickly becomes very popular or well known by being published on the Internet or sent from person to person by e-mail, phone, etc. 病毒式（传播）的
infamy	/'ɪnfəmi/	n.	the state of being well known for sth. bad or evil 臭名昭著；声名狼藉
lurid	/'lʊərɪd/	adj.	shocking and violent in a way that is deliberate 骇人听闻的；令人毛骨悚然的

85

lampoon /læm'pu:n/ v. to criticize sb./sth. publicly in an amusing way that makes them look ridiculous 嘲讽；讥讽

Notes

1. **Memorial Day** is a holiday in the U.S., usually the last Monday in May, in honor of members of the armed forces who have died in war.（美国）阵亡将士纪念日
2. **Ryan Reynolds** (1976–) is a Canadian actor known as the star of the superhero franchise *Deadpool*. 瑞安·雷诺兹（加拿大演员）
3. *Deadpool* is a 2016 superhero film, based on the Marvel Comics antihero of the same name. 电影《死侍》
4. **Eras Tour** is the name of Taylor Swift's concert series in 2023, featuring songs from all her albums. 泰勒·斯威夫特 "Eras" 世界巡回演唱会
5. *Ghostbusters: Frozen Empire* is a sequel to the original *Ghostbusters* movie, featuring the Spengler family and the original team. 电影《捉鬼敢死队：冰冻帝国》
6. *Dune: Part Two* is the sequel to the sci-fi epic *Dune*, directed by Denis Villeneuve and starring Timothée Chalamet, Zendaya, and Rebecca Ferguson. 电影《沙丘2》
7. **SNL**, short for *Saturday Night Live*, is an American late-night live sketch comedy show created by Lorne Michaels and Dick Ebersol, beginning as NBC's Saturday Night on October 11, 1975. The show revolves around sketches parodying current events, American culture, and politics. NBC 周六夜现场

Exercise

Listen to the news report and answer the following questions.

1. What are some of the factors contributing to the decline in box office numbers?
2. What strategies have movie studios adopted to attract audiences back to the theaters?
3. According to Paul Dergarabedian, is the opening weekend of *Dune: Part Two* successful? Why?
4. Since streaming is becoming more and more popular, is it the most important factor that leads to a theatrical meltdown?
5. Did the box office meet people's expectation during last year's Memorial Day weekend?

Entertainment

Part E Projects

Choose one of the following projects, or design one of your own, concerning the theme of this unit. Finish the project by giving a presentation on it in class and chairing a discussion afterwards.

1. Work with your classmates to research Chinese individuals who have made significant contributions to promoting cultural exchanges with other countries. Utilize relevant books and online resources to gather detailed information about who they are, what they did, and the achievements they accomplished.

2. Work in groups of ten to conduct a survey by asking your friends and parents to fill out a questionnaire. The questionnaire should cover the following topics: their preferred forms of entertainment, the types of sports they enjoy, the games they usually play, and their ways of socializing. After gathering the results, compare and summarize how different generations entertain and socialize, and explore the reasons behind these differences.

3. Conduct interviews at a movie theater, asking people if they are attending the theater less frequently. Discuss with them the impact of streaming services on movie theaters and ask them what they believe makes a movie great.

UNIT 9 Business

Part A　The Collapse of the Silicon Valley Bank

 Vocabulary Preparation

bank run			a panic occurring to the bank or banking industry, in which depositors rush to it to withdraw deposits for fear of losing their money when it collapses 银行挤兑
collapse	/kəˈlæps/	v./n.	to fall down suddenly; the falling down of sth. 坍塌；倒塌；暴跌
contagion	/kənˈteɪdʒən/	n.	the quick spreading of sth. bad by being passed from person to person 传染；蔓延
devastating	/ˈdevəsteɪtɪŋ/	adj.	highly destructive or damaging 极具破坏力的；毁灭性的
epicenter	/ˈepɪsentə(r)/	n.	originally referring to the part of the Earth's surface right above the focus of an earthquake; can be used metaphorically as the center of change, reforms, etc. 震中；中心
go under			to be destroyed, defeated, or overwhelmed 被摧毁；被击败
panic	/ˈpænɪk/	n.	a situation where widespread great fear among people causes them to act quickly and without thinking carefully 恐慌；惊恐
ripple effect			a situation where an event or action causes a second event, then a third event, and so on 涟漪作用；连锁反应
slam	/slæm/	v.	to shut sth. with a lot of force（用力）关；砰地关上
Treasury	/ˈtreʒəri/	n.	financial bonds issued by the United States government in order to raise money（美国政府发行的）国库券

 Notes

1. **Coy Wire** (1978–) is an American television anchor and correspondent, and former professional football player in the National Football League. He is currently the anchor of CNN 10. 科伊·怀尔

2. **Silicon Valley Bank** used to be a commercial bank in the San Francisco Bay Area. It collapsed on March 10, 2023, following a bank run triggered by rising interest rates during the 2021–2023 inflation crisis. 硅谷银行

3. **The Federal Deposit Insurance Corporation (FDIC)** is a United States government corporation that provides deposit insurance for depositors in American commercial banks and savings banks. 美国联邦存款保险公司

4. **Signature Bank** used to be an American commercial bank headquartered in New York City. It was taken over by Signature Bridge Bank in 2023 following the collapse of Silicon Valley Bank. This marked the third-largest bank failure in U.S. history. 签名银行

Exercise 1

Listen to the news report and get the main idea.

What is the main point of the news report?

A. Bank panic is contagious among depositors.

B. Joe Biden delivered a speech to ease a bank panic.

C. Silicon Valley Bank collapsed, with people worrying about their deposits.

D. Silicon Valley Bank is saved from collapse because of government bailout.

Exercise 2

Listen to the news report again and fill in the blanks with the exact words or phrases.

Coy Wire: …with the collapse of a bank in the United States over the weekend that has people worried about losing their money and businesses on the verge of going under. Silicon Valley Bank, an epicenter for tech start-up companies with **1.** _____ in deposits at the end of 2022, has collapsed. One reason, those rapidly rising interest rates we've been talking so much about on this show.

Well, they made the Treasuries, in which the bank had invested money, less valuable. So, the bank started to sell them **2.** _____, and that scared people who had money there. So, they went on what's called a bank run, withdrawing all their money in a panic. The more people that did that, the more others wanted to do the same. Inevitably, the bank **3.** _____ .

The FDIC, or Federal Deposit Insurance Corporation, seized control of the bank, and President Biden said yesterday that all 4. _____ would get their money back. And businesses that kept assets there, well, they would have money to pay their employees.

The collapse of Silicon Valley Bank had a ripple effect on a second bank. The same sort of 5. _____ hit Signature Bank shortly after. It had its doors slammed shut, as regulators warned that keeping it open could threaten the entire financial system's 6. _____.

Now, there are fears that other banks may be next. There's a term for this sort of spread of fear over people losing money when banks collapse. It's called contagion. So yesterday morning, President Biden addressed the nation for the first time publicly to try to 7. _____, knowing that the panic could cause a devastating economic fallout for people and businesses around the world.

Joe Biden: All customers who had deposits in these banks can rest assured, I want them to rest assured, they'll be protected, and they'll have access to their money as of today. That includes small businesses across the country that 8. _____ and need to make payroll, pay their bills, and stay open for business.

No losses will be—and this is an important point—no losses will be borne by the taxpayers. Let me repeat that. No losses will be borne by the taxpayers. Instead, the money will come from the fees that banks pay into the deposit insurance fund.

Because of the actions of that—because of the actions that our regulators already taken, every American should feel 9. _____ that their deposits will be there if and when they need them. Second, the management of these banks will be fired if the bank is taken over by FDIC; the people running the bank should not work there anymore.

Third, investors in the banks will not be protected. They knowingly took a risk, and when the risk didn't pay off, investors lose their money. That's how 10. _____ works.

And fourth, there are important questions of how these banks got into the circumstance in the first place. We must get the full accounting of what happened and why those responsible can be held accountable.

Business 9

 Part B   How Much Income Is Needed to Buy a Home?

Vocabulary Preparation

equity	/ˈekwəti/	n.	the sum of your assets, for example the value of your house, once your debts have been subtracted from it 资产净值；权益
established	/ɪˈstæblɪʃt/	adj.	(of a person) well known and respected in a job, etc. that he or she has been doing for a long time 著名的；成名的；公认的
forecast	/ˈfɔːkɑːst/	n.	a statement of what is expected to happen in the future, a prediction 预报
listing	/ˈlɪstɪŋ/	n.	a published list, or an item in a published list 目录；（目录上的）一项
mortgage	/ˈmɔːɡɪdʒ/	n.	a loan of money which you get from a bank or savings and loan association in order to buy a house 房屋抵押贷款
prospect	/ˈprɒspekt/	n.	the future, or chances of being successful 前景；前途
suburb	/ˈsʌbɜːb/	n.	an area where people live that is outside the center of a city 郊区；城外
trade-off			the act of balancing two things that you need or want but which are opposed to each other 权衡；妥协；折中
valid	/ˈvælɪd/	adj.	based on sensible reasoning; effective 合理的；有效的

Note

Daryl Fairweather is the chief economist of Redfin.com. During the housing crisis, Daryl worked as a researcher at the Boston Fed. 达里尔·费尔韦瑟

Exercise

Listen to the news report and choose the best answer to each of the following questions.

1. What is the main idea of the news report?

    A. Mortgage rate keeps increasing rapidly.

    B. Economists are forecasting a brighter housing prospect.

C. Housing in the United States is becoming less affordable now.

D. Living in New York City is not a good choice anymore.

2. According to the news report, under what condition can a family afford a mortgage comfortably?

    A. When the mortgage payment is less than 30% of the family monthly income.

    B. When the mortgage payment is less than 13% of the family monthly income.

    C. When the mortgage payment is less than 30% of the family annual income.

    D. When the mortgage payment is less than 13% of the family annual income.

3. Why does the author regard it worthwhile to buy a house if the family is to stay in it for over five years?

    A. The inadequate house inventory means there will be fewer and fewer houses available in the future.

    B. Homeowners pay fewer taxes when selling the house if they stay in that house for over five years.

    C. The property will accumulate enough value to offer a good return on the family's money.

    D. None of the above.

4. Which of the following is NOT the reason why the economist forecasts next year to be a bit better for buyers?

    A. Housing price will decrease.

    B. Households will make larger income.

    C. Mortgage rates have started to fall.

    D. There will be more houses available on the market.

5. Why is there a trade-off for a lot of young people?

    A. Young people haven't established their career goals.

    B. The decision of whether to buy or rent a house is difficult to make.

    C. The decision of whether to live in city centers or suburbs is difficult to make.

    D. The places that have high paying jobs also have high housing prices.

Business 9 UNIT

▶ Part C Chinese Vehicle Manufacturer BYD Unveils New Double-Decker Bus Design

Vocabulary Preparation

diesel	/ˈdiːzl/	n.	a type of heavy oil used as a fuel instead of petrol or gas 柴油
double-decker		n.	a bus that has two levels or decks 双层巴士
		adj.	(only before noun) having two levels or decks（仅用于名词前）双层的
fleet	/fliːt/	n.	a group of planes, buses, taxis, etc. traveling together or owned by the same organization（同一机构或统一调度的）机群；车队
hybrid	/ˈhaɪbrɪd/	adj.	formed by mixing two or more different things, such as electric power and diesel or petrol（油电）混合的；合成的
navigate	/ˈnævɪgeɪt/	v.	to find your position or the position of your ship, plane, car, etc. and the direction you need to go in, for example by using a map 导航；确定（船、飞机、汽车等）的位置和方向
swap	/swɒp/	v.	to give sth. to sb. and receive sth. else in exchange; to start doing someone else's job, etc. while he or she does yours 调换；交换

Notes

1. **Alexander Denis** is a British bus manufacturing company based in Larbert, Scotland. It's the largest bus and coach manufacturer in the United Kingdom. In May 2019, Alexander Dennis was sold to NFI Group and became its subsidiary. 亚历山大·丹尼斯
2. **BYD** is a publicly listed Chinese multinational manufacturing company headquartered in Shenzhen, Guangdong, China. 比亚迪
3. **Frank Thorpe** is the managing director for commercial vehicles of BYD U.K. 弗兰克·索普
4. **Kitty Logan** is a TV news reporter, video journalist, and media trainer. 基蒂·洛根

Exercise

Listen to the news report and decide whether the following statements are true (T) or false (F).

1. London is replacing older models of double-decker buses to meet clean air targets. (　)
2. The key feature of the new double-decker released by BYD is its large inner space. (　)
3. The new blade battery used in the upgraded BYD double-decker version brings safety and better performance, and saves costs. (　)
4. The new BYD vehicle may meet challenges when facing London's narrow streets and heavy traffic. (　)
5. Technology cannot make a difference if BYD fails to change the traditional look of the original red double-decker bus. (　)

Part D Stock Trading Halted After Markets Plunge at Market Open

 Vocabulary Preparation

buoy	/bɔɪ/	v.	to keep sth. floating; to keep prices at a high or acceptable level 漂浮；浮动
circuit breaker			a metaphor for the halt of stock trading when stock price drops dramatically 股市熔断
close	/kləʊz/	v.	to make the work of a store, market, etc. stop for a period of time; to be worth a particular amount at the end of the day's business 关闭；收盘
coronavirus	/kəˈrəʊnəˌvaɪərəs/	n.	a type of airborne virus accounting for 10%–30% of all colds 冠状病毒
cruise line			a company that operates cruise ships 游轮公司
emergency	/ɪˈmɜːdʒənsi/	n.	a sudden serious and dangerous event or situation which needs immediate action to deal with 突发事件；紧急情况

futures	/ˈfjuːtʃəz/	n.	goods or shares that are bought at agreed prices but that will be delivered and paid for at a later time 期货（交易）
kick in			to start or become activated 开始生效；开始运作
the opening bell			the signal of the opening of stock trading 开市钟
trigger	/ˈtrɪɡə(r)/	v.	to make sth. happen suddenly; to cause a device to start functioning 触发；引发

 Notes

1. **Becky Quick** (1972–) is an American television journalist and co-anchor of CNBC's financial news shows *Squawk Box* and *on the Money*. 贝基·奎克

2. **New York Stock Exchange** (NYSE) is an American stock exchange, also the largest stock exchange in the world by market capitalization, in Manhattan, New York City. 纽约证券交易所

3. **Wall Street** is a street in the Financial District of Lower Manhattan in New York City. Because of its representative position in the financial sector, the term "Wall Street" has become a metonymy for the financial markets of the United States as a whole, the American financial services industry, or the Financial District itself. 华尔街

4. **The Dow** is short for Dow Jones Industrial Average (DJIA). 道指（道琼斯工业指数）

5. **S&P 500** is short for Standard & Poor's 500 Index, an American stock market index based on the market capitalizations of 500 large companies having common stock listed on the NYSE or NASDAQ. 标普 500（指数）

6. **Savannah Guthrie** (1971–) is an American broadcast journalist and former attorney. She is a main co-anchor of the NBC News morning show *Today*. 萨凡纳·格思里

7. **Exxon Mobil** is an American multinational oil and gas corporation headquartered in Irving, Texas, the United States. 埃克森美孚

8. **Chevron**, also Chevron Corporation, is an American multinational energy corporation, headquartered in San Ramon, California. 雪弗龙

9. **The Coronavirus** (COVID-19) is a contagious disease caused by the coronavirus SARS-CoV-2. Its contagious nature and early cause of deaths result in a global pandemic and lead to near universal disruption of supply chains as well as the exchanges among countries. 新冠病毒肺炎

Exercise

Listen to the news report and answer the following questions.

1. What are the motivations underlining the mechanism of circuit breakers?
2. What are the three conditions for circuit breakers to be triggered?
3. Do you think the circuit breaker is an effective mechanism to alleviate panic selling?
4. What are the industries that are severely hit by the coronavirus and why?
5. Economic events are interrelated. Use the message in the news report to help explain this statement.

Part E   Projects

Choose one of the following projects, or design one of your own, concerning the theme of this unit. Finish the project by giving a presentation on it in class and chairing a discussion afterwards.

1. Provide an example of how an economic event, such as the bankruptcy of a company or bank, an increase in mortgage rates, the shift towards online payments, a sudden rise in unemployment, etc., has impacted your life. Discuss the details of the event, its causes, its consequences, and the lessons we can learn from it.

2. Imagine that you and your friends have just graduated from a university and are planning to start your own business. Consider the industry you want to enter. Analyze the macro-environment (political, economic, social, and technological factors), the industry itself (including suppliers, competitors, and consumer needs), and your competitiveness (for example, by using a SWOT analysis). Define your business model (how your company will generate revenue), outline your budget, and prepare a comprehensive business plan. This plan should be designed to appeal to potential venture capitalists or banks, inviting them to provide start-up financing for your business.

3. Select a target company, whether successful or not, and analyze its business strategies in areas such as management, marketing, finance, public relations, and more. If there is a particular strategy in any of these sectors that stands

out as distinctly successful, share the story with the class and explain what others can learn from it. Conversely, if the company's strategy has been unsuccessful or has led to negative outcomes, offer consulting advice to help the company improve its approach.

UNIT 10 Technology

Part A A Legal Loophole of Driverless Cars

Vocabulary Preparation

penalty	/ˈpenəlti/	n.	a punishment for breaking a law, rule, or contract 处罚，惩罚
swerve	/swɜːv/	v.	to change direction suddenly, especially in order to avoid hitting sb./sth. 突然转向；急转弯
overhaul	/ˈəʊvəhɔːl/	n.	an examination of a machine or system, including doing repairs on it or making changes to it 全面改革；彻底检修
shuttle	/ˈʃʌtl/	v.	to carry people between two places that are close, making regular journeys between the two places（在较近的两地之间定时）往返运送；往来穿梭
fare	/feə(r)/	n.	the money that you pay to travel by bus, plane, taxi, etc. 车费；船费；票价
track	/træk/	n.	a mark left by a person, an animal, or a moving vehicle 足迹，踪迹
guinea pig			a person used in medical or other experiments 实验对象；试验品
accountability	/əˌkaʊntəˈbɪləti/	n.	the quality or state of being accountable 责任；责任心

Notes

1. **GM** is the abbreviation for General Motors. It is the largest carmaker in the United States and home to Buick, Cadillac, GMC, and Chevrolet. 美国通用汽车公司
2. **Cruise** is a leading self-driving car company owned by General Motors.（美国通用）自动驾驶子公司 Cruise
3. **Waymo** is a self-driving car company owned by Google.（谷歌旗下的）自动驾驶公司 Waymo
4. **DMV** is the abbreviation for the Department of Motor Vehicles in the U.S. and Canada. 美国和加拿大的车辆管理局

Technology 10

Exercise 1

Listen to the news report and get the main idea.

What is the main point of the news report?

A. Driverless cars are safer than human drivers.

B. There's a legal loophole regarding driverless cars.

C. Human drivers are being replaced by driverless cars.

D. Driverless cars should not be allowed to be on the road.

Exercise 2

Listen to the news report again and fill in the blanks with the exact words or phrases.

The Anchorman: Also tonight, more and more communities are test driving autonomous cars. But in California, a legal loophole lets driverless vehicles avoid any penalties for traffic violations. Bigad Shaban from our Bay Area NBC station investigates.

Bigad Shaban: Driverless cars have run red lights, **1.** _____ into other vehicles, even swerved into wet cement and other construction zones. Plus these so-called Robotaxis can't exactly take orders from police.

Witness of the Car Accident: Sir, there's no one there.

Bigad Shaban: So, when traffic laws are broken and there's no one behind the wheel, who gets the ticket? In Texas and Arizona, where driverless cars are now common in some neighborhoods, companies that own the vehicles can be **2.** _____. But not in California! Even when driverless cars break the rules of the road, we've learned there's not much law enforcement can do. Here in California, traffic tickets can only be written if there's an actual driver. So no human, no fine.

Michael Stevenson (California Attorney): We are very much in the **3.** _____ of the legal grey area when it comes to driverless cars.

Bigad Shaban: California attorney Michael Stevenson has been **4.** _____ car accident victims for more than a

103

decade. Laws are going to have to change.

Michael Stevenson: Right. Absolutely are. (What) we really need is an overhaul, a new set of laws for driverless cars.

Bigad Shaban: It was August when California regulators gave the green light for GM's Cruise and Google's sister company Waymo to expand and start collecting fares as they 5. _____ passengers across San Francisco. But just two months later, the California DMV determined Cruise posed an unreasonable risk to public safety. Cruise saying the most important thing for us right now is to take steps to rebuild public trust, even if it means doing things that are not uncomfortable or difficult. The company pulled all 400 of its driverless cars in the U.S. off the road. Cruise 6. _____ our interview request, but we did hitch a ride with its main competitor, Waymo, which is now the only driverless fleet in America actively picking up passengers.

Chris Ludwick (Head of the Product Management for Waymo): Not all autonomous vehicle technologies are 7. _____ .

Bigad Shaban: Chris Ludwick heads product management for Waymo. If driverless cars can still make mistakes, what makes you so convinced they're still safe enough to be on the road?

Chris Ludwick: Well, there have been examples pointed out where driverless cars continue to need to improve. When we make an improvement at once, that's fixed in our system and the whole fleet gets better. And so the technology is only getting better from here and it's already really good.

Bigad Shaban: Waymo and Cruise say their own researchers found their driverless cars are in some ways safer than human drivers. Neither company has experienced a single death. Waymo has traveled more than 7 million miles. Cruise, more than 5 million. But some question if that's enough of a(n)

Technology UNIT 10

	8. _____ record, since human drivers on average cause 1 death about every 100 million miles.
Irina Raiku (from Santa Clara University):	I think all of us are still struggling to understand whether they really are safer than human drivers, and in what ways and in what ways they might not be.
Bigad Shaban:	Irina Raiku has the Internet ethics program at Santa Clara University, and says we humans have been forced onto a sort of test course for driverless cars. Other drivers, pedestrians, cyclists are, all of a sudden, now 9. _____.
Irina Raiku:	Absolutely. All of us really, who live in areas where such cars are driving.
Bigad Shaban:	Meanwhile, California's DMV says it is working to update regulations, so the next stop for these driverless cars could be new rules and more 10. _____. Bigad Shaban, NBC News, San Francisco.

▶ Part B Are "Digital Humans" the Wave of the Future with AI?

Vocabulary Preparation

coin	/kɔɪn/	v.	to invent a new word or phrase that other people then begin to use 创造（新词语）
vague	/veɪg/	adj.	not having or giving enough information or details about sth. 含糊的；不具体的
multilingual	/ˌmʌltiˈlɪŋgwəl/	adj.	speaking or using several different languages 说（或用）多种语言的；多语的

Notes

1. **John McCarthy** (1927–2011) was an American computer scientist and cognitive

scientist. McCarthy was one of the founders of the discipline of artificial intelligence. He co-authored the document that coined the term "artificial intelligence (AI)". 约翰·麦卡锡（"人工智能"概念提出者之一）

2. **Influencer-type brand collaboration** is a strategic partnership where brands team up with individuals who have a strong online presence in specific niches. 网红类型的品牌合作

3. **LLM** is the abbreviation for Large Language Model. It is a deep learning algorithm that can recognize, summarize, translate, predict, and generate content using very large datasets. 大语言模型

Exercise

Listen to the news report and choose the best answer to each of the following questions.

1. When was the term "artificial intelligence" coined?

    A. In the 1950s.

    B. In the 1960s.

    C. In the 1970s.

    D. In the 1980s.

2. What technology is integrated with the digital human avatars created by Sum Vivas?

    A. 3D technology.

    B. Voice cloning.

    C. Motion capture.

    D. All of the above.

3. Which of the following is NOT a benefit of utilizing digital humans?

    A. They are tireless.

    B. They can speak multiple languages.

    C. They have immense memory capacity.

    D. They learn conversations randomly.

4. What can we learn about the digital DJ Dex according to the news report?

    A. DJ Dex can work without human management.

    B. DJ Dex is not welcomed by some record labels.

    C. DJ Dex is revolutionizing the performance space.

    D. DJ Dex has performed in a few small cities.

5. What does Rob Sims say about AI's threat to people's jobs?

   A. He is worried about the future labor market.

   B. He believes that AI and humans can work as a team.

   C. He is confident that humans will never be replaced by AI.

   D. He thinks people should accept what is inevitable.

Part C How Artificial Intelligence Changes Consumers' Lives?

Vocabulary Preparation

virtual	/ˈvɜːtʃuəl/	adj.	made to appear to exist by the use of computer software, for example on the Internet 模拟的；虚拟的
cashier	/kæˈʃɪə(r)/	n.	a person whose job is to receive and pay out money in a bank, shop/store, hotel, etc. 出纳员
robotics	/rəʊˈbɒtɪks/	n.	the science of designing and operating robots 机器人科学（或技术）
appliance	/əˈplaɪəns/	n.	a machine that is designed to do a particular thing in the home, such as preparing food, heating, or cleaning 器具；（家用）电器
fundamental	/ˌfʌndəˈmentl/	adj.	serious and very important; affecting the most central and important parts of sth. 十分重大的；基础的
revenue	/ˈrevənjuː/	n.	the money that a company, organization, or government receives from people 收入，收益；税收

Notes

1. **iFLYTEK**, founded in 1999, is a listed company in the Asia-Pacific Region focusing on intelligent speech and technology. 科大讯飞（股份有限公司）

2. **R&D** is the abbreviation for research and development. 研发

3. **X-ray** is a type of radiation that can pass through objects that are not transparent and makes it possible to see inside them. X 射线

Exercise

Listen to the news report and decide whether the following statements are true (T) or false (F).

1. At the beginning of the news report, Stephen Hawking is quoted to prove that AI will greatly benefit human beings. (   )
2. iFLYTEK is one of the companies that manage to become a leader in image recognition. (   )
3. The AI voice technology developed by iFLYTEK has been used in many areas like education, healthcare, home, offices, transportation, and media. (   )
4. According to the news report, the AI system can assist the doctor with some fundamental work and speed up the decision-making process. (   )
5. The iFLYTEK product is intended as a replacement of the existing healthcare system. (   )

Part D China's AI: Competition or Cooperation?

Vocabulary Preparation

herald	/ˈherəld/	v.	to be a sign that sth. is going to happen 是（某事）的前兆；预示
disrupt	/dɪsˈrʌpt/	v.	to make it difficult for sth. to continue in the normal way 中断；打乱
dire	/ˈdaɪə(r)/	adj.	very serious 极其严重的；危急的
envision	/ɪnˈvɪʒn/	v.	to imagine what a situation will be like in the future, especially a situation you intend to work towards 展望；想象
velocity	/vəˈlɒsəti/	n.	the speed of sth. in a particular direction 速度；速率
tipping point			the point at which the number of small changes over a period of time reaches a level where a further small change has a sudden and very great effect on a system or leads to an idea suddenly spreading quickly among a large number of people 引爆点，爆发点

Technology 10

Notes

1. **Marvin Minsky** (1927–2016) is an American cognitive scientist in the field of artificial intelligence, co-founder of the Massachusetts Institute of Technology's AI Laboratory, and author of several texts on AI and philosophy. 马文·明斯基
2. **Ray Kurzweil** (1948–) is an American computer scientist and futurist who has pioneered pattern-recognition technology and proselytized the inevitability of humanity's merger with the technology it created. 雷·库兹韦尔（美国发明家、预言家）
3. **Swarm intelligence** refers to the collective behavior of a group of animals, especially social insects such as ants, bees, and termites, that each follow very basic rules. 群体智能

Exercise

Listen to the news report and answer the following questions.

1. According to the speaker, what does "the singularity" mean?
2. What role is China expected to play by 2030 according to the Next Generation Artificial Intelligence Development Plan issued by China's State Council?
3. Which six factors drive China's AI strategy?
4. What advantages does China have in developing AI?
5. Do you agree with the idea that AI has become a kind of battleground between China and the U.S.? Provide evidence for your argument.

Part E Projects

Choose one of the following projects, or design one of your own, concerning the theme of this unit. Finish the project by giving a presentation on it in class and chairing a discussion afterwards.

1. China is making significant strides in AI development, garnering substantial media attention. You are expected to research both print and electronic media to gather more information on the recent advancements in AI technology in China. Your presentation should include an overview of China's achievements in AI development so far, a focus on a specific area with detailed examples, and your thoughts on the future prospects of AI development in China.

2. Since its launch in 2022, ChatGPT has gained popularity across various professions. However, in the field of education, educators remain cautious about its use. What if students use ChatGPT to commit plagiarism? How can teachers detect if plagiarism has occurred? Prepare a report on how students can use ChatGPT responsibly while upholding academic integrity.

3. The breakthrough in AI technology is both inspiring and intimidating. Some people worry that AI is so powerful that it could put many people out of work. Do you think this threat is real? If so, what can people do about it? Identify the professions most likely to be replaced by AI and offer suggestions to help prevent massive unemployment.

UNIT 11 Literature

Part A The "Dan Brown" of Chinese Literature Makes U.S. Debut

Vocabulary Preparation

thrilling	/ˈθrɪlɪŋ/	adj.	causing great excitement or pleasure; very exciting 令人激动的；令人兴奋的
a heck of			a very large amount or number of sth. 非常多
formulaic	/ˌfɔːmjuˈleɪɪk/	adj.	using or involving a fixed or conventional pattern or formula; lacking originality 公式化的；老套的
prose	/prəʊz/	n.	written or spoken language in its ordinary form, without metrical structure 散文
spectacularly	/spekˈtækjələli/	adv.	in a way that is very impressive or striking 壮观地；令人印象深刻地
phenomenally	/fəˈnɒmɪnəli/	adv.	to an extraordinary extent or degree 非凡地；显著地

Notes

1. **Dan Brown** (1964–) is an American author known for writing best-selling thriller novels, often involving a mix of fact and fiction, with recurring themes of conspiracy and religious symbolism. His most famous work is *The Da Vinci Code*. 丹·布朗（美国作家，《达·芬奇密码》作者）

2. **Jorge Luis Borges** (1899–1986) was an Argentine short-story writer, essayist, poet, and translator, known for his short stories that blend fantasy, reality, and philosophical ideas. He is considered one of the most important and influential writers of the 20th century. 豪尔赫·路易斯·博尔赫斯（阿根廷文学家）

3. **Chicken and egg problem** is an informal phrase that describes the cause-and-effect dilemma of determining which of two events is the cause and which is the effect. It is often used to describe situations where it is difficult to determine which came first. "先有鸡还是先有蛋"问题

Literature 11 UNIT

Exercise 1

Listen to the news report and get the main idea.

What is the main point of the news report?

A. It focuses on the comparison between Mai Jia and Dan Brown, emphasizing their similar writing styles.

B. It highlights the difficulties and eventual success of Mai Jia, a Chinese author, in entering the Western publishing market.

C. It discusses the popularity of Chinese television series and films based on Mai Jia's novels.

D. It explores the growth of the Chinese literary market and its influence on Western literature.

Exercise 2

Listen to the news report again and fill in the blanks with the exact words or phrases.

Zafar Anjum: Here's a thrilling story about a Chinese thriller writer who 1. _____ are calling the "Dan Brown" of Chinese literature. Five million copies sold in Chinese, but Western publishers just weren't interested, at least for a while. *WSJ*'s Anna Russell joins us now to explain how it all ended happily, and happy ending is always good with it, with a, with a(n) 2. _____, isn't it? Tell us some.... Tell us more about this author, Mai Jia.

Anna Russell: Mai Jia is a huge author in China. His books have sold over five million copies, altogether.

Zafar Anjum: Five million! I'm told that only 1% of books are more than 5,000 copies. So, five million is a heck of a lot.

Anna Russell: Yes, he's a(n) 3. _____ in China. He's won some of their biggest literary awards, and three out of four of his novels have been made into a television 4. _____ or a film or both.

Zafar Anjum: Now, his typical, his thrillers, don't follow the typical, you know, the typical sort of formulaic thriller writing thing. How do they work?

Anna Russell: Right! So, it's not a traditional Western spy thriller. It's slow moving. It's an in-depth character study. There's a lot of 5. _____ portraits, and it's kind of dense, very literary prose. It's, it's more in the way

113

		of Jorge Luis Borges than Dan Brown, actually.
Zafar Anjum:		But, but, but just as, just as spectacularly successful. Now there's a chicken and egg problem here for Western publishers, and Western publishers don't often speak Chinese or read it, which is the more important thing. So, how do you get a(n) 6. _____ successful book in China that's written in Chinese to a Western publisher and get them to buy it?
Anna Russell:		So, it's very difficult for a(n) 7. _____ Chinese novel to actually get published in the U.S. or the U.K. in English, mainly because it's difficult for the Chinese author to pay for the whole translation themselves before they can be sure of a publishing deal because usually the publisher will pay for the translation once they've decided to make the deal. But it's kind of a chicken or egg, because, you know, they can't 8. _____ to make the translation until they have a(n) 9. _____ of the deal.
Zafar Anjum:		Okay, Mai Jia's been 10. _____ as a literary phenomenon. Thank you very much.

▶ Part B   What If Robert J. Sawyer Writes a Sci-fi Book About China?

🎤 Vocabulary Preparation

arguably	/ˈɑːgjuəbli/	adv.	used to indicate that sth. is possibly true, but that there is room for doubt or for argument 可以说；有争议地
one-off	/ˈwʌnɒf/	adj.	happening only once; not repeated 一次性的；不重复的
subsequent	/ˈsʌbsɪkwənt/	adj.	following in time, order, or place 随后的；接踵而至的
nominate	/ˈnɒmɪneɪt/	v.	formally propose as a candidate or for membership 推荐；提名
ascendancy	/əˈsendənsi/	n.	the state of being superior or dominant 优势；支配地位

curricula	/kəˈrɪkjələ/	n.	(pl.) the subjects comprising an educational course 课程（设置）
prerequisite	/ˌpriːˈrekwəzɪt/	n.	a thing that is required as an essential condition for sth. else to happen or be done 先决条件
supremacy	/suːˈpreməsi/	n.	the state of being superior to all others in authority, power, or status 最高地位；至高无上
be inclined to			to have a tendency or preference for sth. 倾向于；有……的倾向

Notes

1. **Robert J. Sawyer** (1960–) is a Canadian science fiction writer known for his thought-provoking novels that often explore the ethical and philosophical implications of scientific and technological advancements. 罗伯特·J. 索耶（加拿大科幻小说作家）

2. *Star Trek* is a popular science fiction entertainment franchise that began with a television series created by Gene Roddenberry. It has since expanded into films, books, and other media, depicting a future where humanity explores space and encounters new civilizations.《星际迷航》

3. **Hard science fiction** is a subgenre of science fiction that emphasizes scientific accuracy and technical details in its storytelling, often exploring the potential consequences of scientific and technological advancements. 硬科幻小说

4. **The Three Gorges Dam** is the world's largest hydroelectric dam that spans the Yangtze River in China. 三峡大坝

5. **The Terracotta Warriors** are a collection of terracotta sculptures depicting the armies of Qin Shi Huang, the first emperor of China. They were buried with the emperor in 210 B.C.–209 B.C. and were discovered in 1974 near Xi'an, Shaanxi Province. 兵马俑

6. **Kim Stanley Robinson** (1952–) is an American author, known for his science fiction works that often explore themes of environmentalism, technology, and the future of humanity. His most acclaimed work is the *Mars Trilogy*. 金·斯坦利·罗宾逊（美国作家）

Exercise

Listen to the news report and choose the best answer to each of the following questions.

1. Who is referred to as "Canada's godfather of science fiction"?
   A. Liu Cixin.

B. Kim Stanley Robinson.

   C. Robert J. Sawyer.

   D. Hai Ya.

2. What recent honor was mentioned regarding Liu Cixin in the news report?

   A. He won another Hugo Award.

   B. He received the Nobel Prize in Literature.

   C. He was nominated for the Nebula Award.

   D. He had a starship named after him on *Star Trek*.

3. What type of science fiction do Robert J. Sawyer and Liu Cixin write?

   A. Fantasy science fiction.

   B. Hard science fiction.

   C. Soft science fiction.

   D. Cyberpunk science fiction.

4. Which museum did Robert J. Sawyer express a desire to visit, mentioned by the reporter?

   A. The Zigong Dinosaur Museum.

   B. The Shanghai History Museum.

   C. The Palace Museum.

   D. The Guangzhou Museum.

5. What advice does Robert J. Sawyer give to Chinese science fiction writers?

   A. They should focus on writing fantasy rather than science fiction.

   B. They should imitate Western writers to gain popularity.

   C. They should tell their own stories deeply rooted in Chinese culture.

   D. They should write about historical events.

Part C   Tanzania's Abdulrazak Gurnah Wins 2021 Nobel Prize for Literature

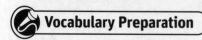

| prank | /præŋk/ | *n.* | a playful or mischievous trick 恶作剧 |

uncompromising	/ʌnˈkɒmprəmaɪzɪŋ/	adj.	determined not to make concessions or to accept anything less than what is desired 毫不妥协的；坚定的
compassionate	/kəmˈpæʃənət/	adj.	feeling or showing sympathy and concern for others' suffering 有同情心的；表示同情的
persecution	/ˌpɜːsɪˈkjuːʃn/	n.	the action of subjecting sb. to cruelty or unfair treatment because of their beliefs or way of life 迫害
meanness	/ˈmiːnnəs/	n.	the quality of being unkind or ungenerous 吝啬；小气
empty-handed	/ˌemptiˈhændɪd/	adj.	without having achieved what one was trying to achieve 空手的；未成功的
prevalence	/ˈprevələns/	n.	the fact of being very common at a particular time or in a particular place 普遍性；流行
laureate	/ˈlɒriət/	n.	a person who has been officially recognized for his/her achievements, especially in literature, and has received an honor or prize 获奖者；荣誉获得者

 Notes

1. **Tanzania** is a country in East Africa, known for its diverse landscapes, wildlife, and rich cultural heritage. It is home to Mount Kilimanjaro, Africa's highest peak, and the Serengeti National Park, famous for its annual migration of wildebeest. 坦桑尼亚

2. **Abdulrazak Gurnah** (1948–) is a novelist and scholar from Zanzibar, Tanzania, who won the Nobel Prize in Literature in 2021. His works often explore themes of colonialism, migration, and the experiences of individuals caught between cultures. 阿卜杜勒拉扎克·古尔纳（坦桑尼亚桑小说家和学者，2021 年获得诺贝尔文学奖）

3. **The Swedish Academy** is an organization in Sweden dedicated to the promotion and preservation of the Swedish language and literature. It is responsible for compiling the official Swedish dictionaries. It is also the body that awards the Nobel Prize in Literature. 瑞典文学院

Exercise

Listen to the news report and decide whether the following statements are true (T) or false (F).

1. Abdulrazak Gurnah received the Nobel Prize in Literature on a Thursday while he was in his kitchen in Zanzibar. (　　)
2. Abdulrazak Gurnah is the first black African to win the Nobel Prize in Literature. (　　)
3. The Swedish Academy has faced criticism for being too Western-centric and male-oriented. (　　)
4. Gurnah's novels include *Afterlives* and *Paradise*, the latter of which was shortlisted for the Booker Prize. (　　)
5. The sudden fame of Abdulrazak Gurnah as the 2021 Nobel laureate has not influenced the demand for his books. (　　)

Part D University Launches Taylor Swift-Inspired Literature Course

Vocabulary Preparation

icon	/ˈaɪkɒn/	n.	a famous person or thing that people admire and see as a symbol of a particular idea, way of life, etc. 偶像；崇拜对象
kick off			to start sth., such as a meeting or an event 开始；启动
tease out			to extract or draw out gradually or with effort 逐渐提取；仔细梳理
shake off			to get rid of sb./sth. that is following or clinging to you 摆脱；抖落
pull off			to achieve sth. difficult, especially in a way that is impressive 完成；成功做到

Notes

1. **Taylor Swift** (1989–) is an American singer-songwriter known for her narrative songwriting, which often incorporates autobiographical elements and emotional responses to personal experiences. She has won numerous awards and is one of the best-selling music artists of all time. 泰勒·斯威夫特

2. ***Jane Eyre***, a novel by Charlotte Bronte published in 1847, follows the life of a young orphan in 19th-century England who becomes a governess and ultimately finds love. The novel delves into themes of morality, religion, and societal expectations.《简·爱》

3. ***Romeo and Juliet*** is a tragedy by William Shakespeare about two young star-crossed lovers whose deaths ultimately reconcile their feuding families. It is a play that explores themes of love, fate, and the consequences of family conflict.《罗密欧与朱丽叶》

4. ***Alice in Wonderland***, a novel by Lewis Carroll first published in 1865, follows a young girl named Alice as she falls down a rabbit hole into a whimsical world inhabited by peculiar creatures. It is renowned for its playfulness, wordplay, and exploration of logic and philosophy.《爱丽丝梦游仙境》

Exercise

Listen to the news report and answer the following questions.

1. What new course is being introduced in Europe, inspired by Taylor Swift?
2. What themes in English literature classics are also being present in Taylor Swift's songs?
3. From which song does the reporter Bradley Harris quote the lyrics during the conversation?
4. What method does the lecturer Ellie McCausland use to discuss Taylor Swift's songs in the course?
5. What humorous remark does Bradley Harris make at the end of the conversation?

Part E Projects

Choose one of the following projects, or design one of your own, concerning the theme of this unit. Finish the project by giving a presentation on it in class and chairing a discussion afterwards.

1. Explain how Nobel Prize laureates in literature are selected. Start by outlining the role and structure of the Swedish Academy, examining the nomination and selection process, identifying the criteria for evaluating literary works, and exploring the influence of cultural and political considerations. Then, provide

your commentary on the system. Do you believe it is a fair way of selecting laureates? You may use recent examples, such as Abdulrazak Gurnah, to support your argument.

2. There are numerous science fiction traditions worldwide, but two stand out: the Chinese tradition, represented by authors like Liu Cixin, and the Western tradition, represented by authors like Robert J. Sawyer. While these two traditions share many similarities, each also possesses distinct qualities. Your project will focus on these similarities and differences. Please compare the themes, cultural influences, and narrative styles of Chinese science fiction with those of Western science fiction.

3. Many students find literature courses boring or irrelevant. There are various ways to make these courses more engaging, such as incorporating multimedia resources, connecting themes to current events, and using interactive activities. Should traditional methods be replaced with these new approaches? Share your opinions with your classmates.

UNIT 12 Nature

Part A Fire Season in Australia

Vocabulary Preparation

spell	/spel/	v.	to have sth., usually sth. bad, as a result 招致；意味着（通常指坏事）
habitat	/ˈhæbɪtæt/	n.	the place where a particular type of animal or plant is normally found（动植物的）生活环境；栖息地
bushfire	/ˈbʊʃfaɪə(r)/	n.	fire in the forest 林区大火
spark	/spɑːk/	v.	to cause sth. to start or develop, especially suddenly 引发；触发
trailer	/ˈtreɪlə(r)/	n.	a truck, or a container with wheels, that is pulled by another vehicle 拖车；挂车
pump	/pʌmp/	n.	a machine that is used to force liquid, gas, or air into or out of sth. 抽水机；泵
recruit	/rɪˈkruːt/	n.	a person who joins an organization, a company, etc. 新成员
deploy	/dɪˈplɔɪ/	v.	to use sth. effectively 有效利用；调动
brag	/bræɡ/	v.	to talk too proudly about sth. you own or sth. you have done 吹嘘；自吹自擂

Notes

1. **Australia's bushfires** refer to wildfires that occur in its bushland areas. The 2019–2020 fire season, known as Black Summer, was particularly severe, with fires burning millions of acres, destroying homes, and decimating wildlife populations. 澳大利亚丛林火灾

2. **The Rural Fire Service (RFS)** is a volunteer-based firefighting agency and statutory body of the Government of New South Wales in Australia. The RFS is responsible for the majority of rural firefighting, and it is the largest volunteer fire service in the world.（澳大利亚）乡村消防服务

3. **New South Wales** is one of the states of Australia, located in the southeastern part of the country along the coast. It is the most populous state in Australia and includes the most populous city, Sydney. 新南威尔士

4. **Picton Rural Fire Brigade** is a brigade within the New South Wales Rural Fire Service, indicating that this interview takes place in New South Wales. 皮克顿乡村消防队

Nature 12 UNIT

Exercise 1

Listen to the news report and get the main idea.

What is the main point of the news report?

A. Volunteer firefighting in Australia is important and challenging.

B. The first thing a new firefighter needs to learn is how to operate a pump.

C. Global warming and El Niño are causing extreme summer heat and fires in Australia.

D. The New South Wales Rural Fire Service was founded in 1939 by local farmers and residents.

Exercise 2

Listen to the news report again and fill in the blanks with the exact words or phrases.

Coy Wire: Experts worry that the combination of El Niño and the underlying global heating spells a summer of extreme heat and fire. Australia **1.** _____ its worst fires in 2019 and 2020, burning millions of acres, including homes and natural **2.** _____. The fire season down under usually starts in October and ends around March. It's a dangerous, sometimes deadly time for people and wildlife. Already this year, **3.** _____ have hit parts of the country and firefighters are working hard to keep up with the help of volunteer crews. There are tens of thousands of volunteer firefighters across Australia, especially in rural areas. We're about to join two of them now.

Lauren Wilson (Advance Firefighter): When I tell people I'm a firefighter, I actually get a lot of mixed reactions. Oh, you do all that for free? What makes you do that? It really does **4.** _____ a lot of curiosity in people.

Coy Wire: Australia battles some of the largest and hottest wildfires on the planet. The fire season in Australia typically runs from October until the end of March, when temperatures are at their highest. Most of the firefighting is conducted by the Rural Fire Service, a volunteer force separate to state emergency services. The New South Wales Rural Fire Service has more than 70,000 members.

Andrew Hain (Senior Deputy Captain, Picton Rural Fire Brigade Internal Flight

	Planner): We were founded in 1939 by local farmers and local residents that needed a firefighting service in the area, and it was a bunch of guys with old trucks or **5.** _____. Now we're sitting here in a-million-dollar-plus facility with these trucks that are basically a(n) **6.** _____. We do flood work in this. We do fires, car accidents, house fires.
Lauren Wilson:	We're coming into a family of a long line of firefighters. I believe there is that little bit of pressure. I can remember when I first told my **7.** _____ that I had joined, the first thing he said to me was, "As long as you can operate a pump, you'll be fine."
Coy Wire:	As a volunteer service, **8.** _____ come from all walks of life and require intense training before being deployed.
Andrew Hain:	It's a huge amount of effort. A lot of hours go into training a new recruit. It's not for **9.** _____ rights; it's because they've got to go out on the truck with you. You need to be able to work with everybody from different backgrounds. You know, people that work in corporate, people that work in **10.** _____, you'd name it. We've probably got it.

▶ Part B How Climate Change Is Impacting Antarctica?

Vocabulary Preparation

expedition	/ˌekspəˈdɪʃn/	n.	a journey or voyage undertaken by a group of people with a particular purpose, especially that of exploration 探险；考察
intrepid	/ɪnˈtrepɪd/	adj.	very brave, fearless, unshaken 无畏的；勇敢的
elusive	/iˈluːsɪv/	adj.	difficult to find, catch, or achieve 难以捉摸的
otherworldly	/ˌʌðəˈwɜːldli/	adj.	related to an imaginary or spiritual world 超凡脱俗的；超自然的
endurance	/ɪnˈdjʊərəns/	n.	the ability to endure an unpleasant or difficult process or situation without giving way 耐力；承受力
glacial	/ˈɡleɪʃl/	adj.	relating to, resulting from, or denoting the presence or agency of ice, especially in the form of glaciers 冰川的

majestic	/məˈdʒestɪk/	adj.	having or showing impressive beauty or scale 壮丽的；雄伟的
accelerating	/əkˈselərettɪŋ/	adj.	increasing speed, amount, or extent 加速的
breathtaking	/ˈbreθteɪkɪŋ/	adj.	extremely exciting, beautiful, or surprising 激动人心的；惊人的
rookery	/ˈrʊkəri/	n.	a breeding place or colony of certain birds and animals, especially rooks, penguins, or seals 某些鸟类和动物的繁殖地或群体；群居地
unfazed	/ʌnˈfeɪzd/	adj.	not disconcerted or perturbed 泰然自若的；未受干扰的
orca	/ˈɔːkə/	n.	a large toothed whale that is black above with white underparts and white oval-shaped patches behind the eyes; also known as a killer whale 鲸；虎鲸

 Notes

1. **Antarctica** is a virtually uninhabited, ice-covered landmass located at the South Pole, and is renowned for being the coldest, driest, and windiest continent. 南极洲
2. **Amy Robach** (1973–) is a renowned television presenter for *ABC News*, co-anchoring *20/20* and reporting for *Good Morning America* and other ABC News broadcasts. 艾米·罗巴赫
3. **Lindblad expeditions**, founded by Lars-Eric Lindblad, offers expedition cruises and adventure travel experiences in various parts of the world, including Antarctica. 林德布拉德探险
4. **Crabeater seals** are one of the most populous seal species, native to the pack ice of Antarctica. 食蟹海豹

Exercise

Listen to the news report and choose the best answer to each of the following questions.

1. Where is Amy Robach currently reporting from?
   A. South Africa.　　　　　　　　B. New York City.
   C. The Arctic Circle.　　　　　　D. Lindblad Bay, Antarctica.
2. What is the name of the ship which Amy and her crew are traveling on?

A. Titanic. B. Explorer.
C. Discovery. D. Endurance.

3. Which of the following animals did Amy mention seeing in Antarctica?

    A. Lions. B. Kangaroos.
    C. Polar bears. D. Crabeater seals.

4. What is the impact of climate change on Antarctica, according to Amy's report?

    A. It's causing the animals to migrate to other regions.

    B. It's making the continent colder and creating more ice.

    C. It's making the continent warmer and causing ice to melt.

    D. It's leading to an increase in human population in the region.

5. What was the original plan for Amy's expedition that had to be altered due to the unpredictable conditions of Antarctica?

    A. They were supposed to go hiking.

    B. They were supposed to go on a kayak.

    C. They were supposed to go snowboarding.

    D. They were supposed to go swimming with seals.

Part C Protecting a Forest by Cutting down Christmas Trees

Vocabulary Preparation

ranch	/rɑːntʃ/	n.	a large farm for raising horses, beef cattle, or other livestock 牧场；大农场
bounty	/ˈbaʊnti/	n.	a large amount of sth. that is good or desirable 丰富；大量
aspen	/ˈæspən/	n.	a kind of tree that is related to the poplar and has leaves that move easily in the wind 白杨树
canyon	/ˈkænjən/	n.	a deep valley with steep sides and often with a stream flowing through it 峡谷
underbrush	/ˈʌndəbrʌʃ/	n.	plants, bushes, and small trees growing beneath larger trees in a forest 下层灌丛；灌木丛

Nature 12

bankruptcy	/'bæŋkrʌptsi/	n.	a state of being unable to pay debts 破产
spacing	/'speɪsɪŋ/	n.	the amount of space between things 间隔；间距
wilderness	/'wɪldənəs/	n.	an area of land that has not been used to grow crops or had towns and roads built on it; a wild and natural area 未开发的土地；荒野
reconnect	/ˌriːkə'nekt/	v.	to establish a bond or relationship with sb. again 重新连接；重新建立关系
deployment	/dɪ'plɔɪmənt/	n.	the movement of soldiers or equipment to a place where they can be used when they are needed 部署

Notes

1. **Aspen Canyon Ranch** is a ranch located in Colorado, the United States. 阿斯彭峡谷牧场
2. **The Rocky Mountains**, also known as the Rockies, are a major mountain range in western North America. 落基山山脉
3. **Denver-Based Dolores Project** is a project based in Denver, Colorado, and provides safe, comfortable shelter and personalized services for unaccompanied women and transgender individuals experiencing homelessness. 丹佛多洛雷斯项目
4. **Dude ranch** is a type of ranch oriented towards visitors or tourism. 度假牧场
5. **Colorado State Forest Service** is a service and outreach agency of the Warner College of Natural Resources at Colorado State University. 科罗拉多州森林服务局
6. **Project Sanctuary** is a U.S.-based non-profit organization that aims to help military families reconnect and reintegrate into their communities after service. 庇护项目
7. **CBS News** is an American television broadcast news division owned by the CBS Entertainment Group division of Viacom. 美国电视广播新闻部门

Exercise

Listen to the news report and decide whether the following statements are true (T) or false (F).

1. Aspen Canyon Ranch is in Colorado, where people can choose and cut their own Christmas trees with a donation to the Denver-Based Dolores Project. (   )
2. The Denver-Based Dolores Project is an organization that provides shelter for homeless men. (   )

3. The Aspen Canyon Ranch was previously a dude ranch and then turned into a marijuana B&B before facing bankruptcy. (   )
4. The Colorado State Forest Service is not involved in any of the activities at Aspen Canyon Ranch. (   )
5. Project Sanctuary will not be involved with the ranch after Phillip Xavier completes the tree spacing and underbrush clearing. (   )

Part D   How China's New National Parks Are Protecting Biodiversity?

Vocabulary Preparation

conservation	/ˌkɒnsə'veɪʃn/	n.	the protection of plants and animals, natural areas, and interesting and important structures and buildings, especially from the damaging effects of human activity 保护；保存
preservation	/ˌprezə'veɪʃn/	n.	the act of keeping sth. in its original state or in good condition 保护；保存
flora	/'flɔːrə/	n.	the plants of a particular region, habitat, or geological period 植物群
fauna	/'fɔːnə/	n.	all the animals of a particular region or period 动物群
species	/'spiːʃiːz/	n.	a set of animals or plants in which the members have similar characteristics to each other and can breed with each other 物种；种类
biodiversity	/ˌbaɪəʊdaɪ'vɜːsəti/	n.	the number and variety of plants and animals that exist in a particular area or in the world generally, or the problem of protecting this 生物多样性
ranger	/'reɪndʒə(r)/	n.	a person whose job is to protect forests or natural parks, or a soldier who has been specially trained to fight in difficult conditions 警卫员；护林员
tropical	/'trɒpɪkl/	adj.	from or relating to the area between the two tropics 热带的
topography	/tə'pɒɡrəfi/	n.	the physical shape of the land 地形；地貌

Nature 12 UNIT

patrol	/pəˈtrəʊl/	n.	a person or group of people sent to keep watch over an area, especially a military one 巡逻
infrared	/ˌɪnfrəˈred/	adj.	producing or using rays of light that cannot be seen and that are longer than rays that produce red light 红外线的
urbanize	/ˈɜːbənaɪz/	v.	to make an area more like a city by building houses, shops, etc. on it 城市化；都市化

Notes

1. **Kyle Obermann** is a conservation photographer and writer who has spent seven years traveling through China's most wild and stunning landscapes. 凯尔·奥伯曼
2. **Rose Niu** is the Chief Conservation Officer at the Paulson Institute, an independent research institute that advances environmental conservation. 牛红卫
3. **Himalayas** is a mountain range extending about 2,400 kilometers (1,500 miles) along the border between India and China's Xizang. 喜马拉雅山脉
4. **COP15** refers to the 15th Meeting of the Conference of the Parties (COP) to the Convention on Biological Diversity, held in Kunming, China, in 2021.《生物多样性公约》第十五次缔约方大会

Exercise

Listen to the news report and answer the following questions.

1. Who is Kyle Obermann and what has he been doing in China for the past seven years?
2. How does China's approach to conservation and the creation of national parks differ from other countries, according to Kyle Obermann?
3. According to Rose Niu, why is China's biodiversity so rich and what is the importance of China's achievements in biodiversity conservation and wilderness protection for the future of global biodiversity conservation?
4. What is Sanjiangyuan National Park and who is Liu Yuhan? Can you describe his role and his work done in this park?
5. What is China's position in global biodiversity and wilderness protection according to the last paragraph, and what challenges are mentioned for other countries as they progress economically?

Part E Projects

Choose one of the following projects, or design one of your own, concerning the theme of this unit. Finish the project by giving a presentation on it in class and chairing a discussion afterwards.

1. Using data from various sources, create a biodiversity map of a selected region in China. The map should depict the diversity of flora and fauna, with a focus on endemic and endangered species. Use this map to analyze the current state of biodiversity, identify potential threats to species and their habitats, and evaluate the effectiveness of existing conservation measures. Based on your findings, propose useful strategies to enhance biodiversity conservation in this region.

2. Conduct a study of successful community-based conservation projects in China, such as the involvement of local Tibetans as rangers in Sanjiangyuan National Park. Analyze how these initiatives have contributed to nature conservation and their impact on local communities, including livelihoods and cultural preservation. Based on your findings, design a community-based conservation project that can be implemented in another region, taking into account the specific environmental and social contexts of the area.

3. Research and present how technology is being used to enhance the tourist experience at destinations across China. Focus on innovations such as virtual reality tours of historical sites like the Forbidden City, mobile apps offering navigation and cultural information for places like the Great Wall, and digital pass systems used in large amusement parks like Shanghai Disneyland. Evaluate the effectiveness of these technologies in improving visitor satisfaction and engagement, and propose further improvements or new technologies that could be introduced to enhance the tourism experience in China.

Appendix I Scripts

Unit 1 Education

Part A ChatGPT in the Classroom

George: In our series, The Tech Effect. It's only been a few months since we started hearing about ChatGPT and the AI chatbot is already finding his way in the classrooms. Rebecca Jarvis is back and we're seeing teachers incorporate this technology into their lesson plans.

Rebecca Jarvis: George, this technology is still so new. It comes with plenty of unknowns and it raises some very big questions about plagiarism and cheating, which is why some schools have actually banned it. But other schools are now incorporating ChatGPT into their lesson plans and we got an up-close look at how.

Rebecca Jarvis: These fifth-grade students might look like they're doing an average writing assignment (Teacher: Good. What do you think?), but their prompt wasn't created by their teacher. Instead, they chose from ten different options generated in seconds by ChatGPT, an artificially intelligent chatbot.

Donnie Piercy (Fifth-Grade Teacher, 2021 Kentucky Teacher of the Year): Like every other educator, I had that concern. Is this something that students are only going to use to cheat? So I started to think about like "Okay, what role is AI, artificial intelligence, going to play in the classroom".

Rebecca Jarvis: Kentucky Teacher of the Year, Donnie Piercy, let us peek inside his Lexington fifth-grade class where they utilize ChatGPT in a number of ways from grammar exercises like Find the Bot, where students have to guess which paragraph was written by ChatGPT versus their classmates.

Donnie Piercy: Do any of these jump out, as, like, "Ooh, I'm pretty sure it's not that one"?

Student 1: For the second one, because they put "who invented plethora of inventions", they should have put "a plethora".

Donnie Piercy: Oh, interesting catch there!

Rebecca Jarvis: ...to reading exercises through personalized plays generated in seconds by the program.

Student 2: In a typical fifth-grade classroom, the door bursts open, and a superhero named Super Potato bursts in.

Student 3: Fear not citizens, Super Potato is here to save the day!

Donnie Piercy: So the big thing that I've looked for as a teacher over the last seventeen years is what things I can bring into my lessons that inspire my students to be creative. With AI, with ChatGPT, I've always looked for a way that I can use this tool to inspire my students to become better students to really master content.

Rebecca Jarvis: Many of his students think of it as something that's here to stay.

Girl 1: So if it keeps on expanding, that's basically typical for what this generation is doing right now.

Boy 1: I feel like it can evolve a lot over time.

Boy 2: If you keep AI, like, safe, (it's) going to be really helpful.

Rebecca Jarvis: And it's not just elementary school. Across the country in Oregon, mother and son teachers Tobin and Cherie Shields utilize it at the high school and collegiate level.

Tobin Shields (Computer Information Systems Instructor): It is going to make our educational system more accurate and it's going to make it more interesting and more accessible and more creative, where I think a lot of educators think it's going to do the opposite.

Rebecca Jarvis: Cherie, an educator of thirty years penning an opinion piece for Education Week titled "Don't ban ChatGPT. Use it as a teaching tool".

Cherie Shield (High School English Teacher): I do think employers in the future are going to be asking employees to work with AI. It's just a life skill that we are going to have to perpetuate forward if we want our students to be viable in the workplace.

Rebecca Jarvis: Some very interesting applications there. But of course, there are those very real concerns about cheating, plagiarism, authenticity. OpenAI, the company that created ChatGPT has also created what they call an AI Classifier. That is a program that can essentially decipher whether a text was written by AI or by a human. Many other companies are working on similar programs. George, I predict this piece is going to

	be in a time capsule thirty years from now. Those fifth graders talking about the future. We're going to look at the world so differently because of this technology.
George:	You don't want kids to lose the ability to write.
Rebecca Jarvis:	Exactly and have creativity and come from themselves, not from the machine.
George:	Rebecca, thanks very much.

Part B Future of Education: How Is AI Affecting the Study of the Humanities in China?

Artificial intelligence is transforming the world of education. In China, the cutting-edge technology is being promoted across the board, including at universities, where it's even reshaping the future of arts students. CGTN's Lu Sirui spoke to professors working in the humanities and the AI center at one of China's elite universities.

The patterns on these antiques tell a story. That's according to a professor in the Archeology Departments at China's Peking University. He says the evolution of these patterns can offer insights into the spread of culture across place and time.

Before, it might take years for researchers to find and piece together the information, matching evolutionary outcomes with certain patterns. But now the results are practically immediate, all at the tip of the fingers.

Zhang Hai (President, School of Archaeology and Museology, Peking University): In fact, image analysis is very personal. This AI software will correct and assist according to the researcher's logic, and ultimately provide personalized services.

The professor says AI has been already applied in archeological research for many years, but it's now on the verge of becoming more accessible to students and early career researchers.

Zhang Hai (President, School of Archaeology and Museology Peking University): We now have a lot of contents, such as the study of quantitative archeology and spatial analysis, which all involve the use of AI. In the future, after these contents are more systematic, we may open a new course.

The wide appliance of AI technology across many industries has already raised deep philosophical questions and posed serious ethical issues.

New interdisciplinary courses are expected to open between philosophy and other subjects, creating new opportunities for philosophy majors outside the university, especially in the field of AI ethics.

Sebastian Sunday Grève (Assistant Professor, Department of Philosophy, Peking University): We need to learn how to integrate this new technology. That means how to develop it in such a way that it will not be harmful to society. We also need to educate ourselves how to act and interact in relation to it. The new world of social media is indeed one battlefield as it's often described where we do interact with AI and on the basis of AI. So, these are areas in which philosophy graduates can be more hopeful to find job opportunities in the future.

Lin Zhouchen (Professor, School of Intelligence Science and Technology, Peking University): We have the Artificial Intelligence Research Institute, which specializes in intersecting artificial intelligence and other disciplines, including humanities. We are dedicated to enable machines acting autonomously, based on correct values, and help the humanities to carry out systematic upgrades and accelerate their scientific research process.

Lu Sirui: Professors also said that the use of artificial intelligence is very similar to the acceptance of computers decades ago. So it's very important for the schools to equip the students with the skill, and prepare them for the future world that will be reshaped by the technology. Lu Sirui, CGTN, Beijing.

Part C No Smartphones on Campus

Coy Wire: Question for you. How would you feel about going to a school where they don't allow any smartphones on campus? Maybe that's already the case for some of you. But if not, how would you feel about being away from your phone for eight hours or so each day? If you like the idea, why? If not, what would be your reasoning for the objection? Our CNN Digital Team went to one small high school in Massachusetts where they don't allow smartphones so we could learn why the school did it and what the outcome has been.

Unidentified Female: Buxton School, a small private boarding school for grades 9 to 12 in Massachusetts, banned smartphones on campus back in 2022.

John Kalapos (Co-director): It was absolute chaos.

Owen (Senior): Oh boy.

Noelle: People thought it was a joke at first.

John Kalapos: They were not happy. Parents were calling us.

Noelle:	There was a lot of, like, "I can't live without my phone."
Unidentified Female:	Students tell CNN that they know this place is special. Buxton isn't like many other schools. It's home to only 55 students, many living full-time on campus away from their families, making this a tight-knit community. Plus, the school practices progressive education. That means teachers don't track test scores or grades. But just like more traditional high schools, teachers at Buxton were struggling to hold students' attention. Kids were glued to their screens.
Kalapos:	It was a lot of little things, right? It's that when you're teaching a lesson and you can tell that half the class is, like, discreetly looking under their desk at something. It's walking into a lunchroom and seeing half the lunchroom scrolling on TikToks instead of talking to their friends. It's walking down the path, everyone's looking down, everyone's not looking up.
Unidentified Female:	That is, until administration banned smartphones on campus about a year and a half ago.
Noelle:	I've been more social, like, naturally instead of being, like, forced to be social.
Owen:	People were more there at the meals. I mean, I was sitting with people I didn't sit with before, with new groups of people and, you know, talking to all these new people.
Nori Junior:	This is from earlier and, like, Iris drew this part without seeing any of this and then Jasper drew this part and then we opened it up and see, like, what we made all together.
Owen:	Last night we had a dorm party.
Kalapos:	We have a black and white photography program here. That photo program went from 12 students to 35 students because now everyone's carrying a 35mm camera and printing in the darkroom.
Owen:	The initial idea of no phones felt a lot more intense than actually not having phones. It was more like no access to social media all the time in your pocket.
Unidentified Female:	Most of the students CNN interviewed welcomed the change of pace brought on by the smartphone ban. But the jury's still out for some.

Nori:	I sort of have the opinion that it was not a good idea to ban phones. If you don't get practice with phones, they are designed to be so addictive. They're not getting practice using their phones while going to school and stuff like that.
Noelle:	I mean, we still have iPads, we still have computers. People can have flip phones. Like, I think a lot of people are like, the world is going to end. I don't know how I'm going to survive without my phone. And I think as time goes on, people have adapted to like using a computer. Like I've sent a lot more emails since I've gotten better at emailing.
Owen:	I feel like there's this pressure to have a presence online and to be active with your presence online and do all this stuff online. After not having a phone and not being able to keep up with that always, I find that that's not needed. Phones are overrated. Definitely.

Part D Tuition-Free

Ruth Gottesman:	I'm happy to share with you that starting in August this year, the Albert Einstein College of Medicine will be tuition-free.
News Anchor:	That's what you call—having a good day. A big deal for hundreds of medical students right here in the Bronx, New York. Tuition alone at Albert Einstein College is more than $59,000 a year. That's a lot of money. Now, a massive donation from a long-time professor will cover that cost. Our lead national correspondent David Begnaud has more on yesterday's announcement. David?
News Anchor:	Hey, it's good to see you. We haven't seen you in the studio in a long time, but what a great story!
David Begnaud:	So good to be with you all. I feel like I was one of them yesterday. I was as excited as they were right just hearing this news. Good morning to all of you. The gift is going to transform the lives of these students and will allow these future doctors to begin their careers without medical-school debts. The donation totals $1 billion. It is the largest donation ever to a medical school in the country. Here's how the gift will work. Beginning in August of this year, all current and future students will receive free tuition. Current fourth-year students will be reimbursed for their Spring Semester. If you're wondering

	what this means for the students, here's Trevor Barker, talking about what went through his mind when he heard about the gift.
Trevor Barker:	For a minute, I was just staring blankly, like I was processing. But then I started to think about what it could mean for my family and taking care of my mom throughout medical school and being able to take care of her after I graduate financially.
David Begnaud:	What a blessing. Now the donor behind this gift is 93-year-old Ruth Gottesman. She's also the one who made the announcement to the students in that video. She is currently chair of the college's board of trustees and she was a former professor at the school. Gottesman joined the college in 1968 as part of its Children's Evaluation and Rehabilitation Center, where she developed screening and treatment techniques for children with learning disabilities. The donation is named…is made in the name of her late husband David. He was a notable businessman who was an early investor in Berkshire Hathaway and actually the protege of Warren Buffett. And guys, he said to her in his will—with this money, do what you think is right.
News Anchor:	Hmm, right, that's what she did. What a difference she's made!

Unit 2 People

Part A Martin Luther King's Legacy

Yolanda Renee King:	If I could speak to my grandfather today, I would say I'm sorry we still have to be here, to rededicate ourselves to finishing your work and ultimately realizing your hidden dream.
Martha:	That was Dr. Martin Luther King Jr.'s only grandchild, 15-year-old Yolanda Renee King, marking the 60th anniversary of the March on Washington this weekend. ABC's chief justice correspondent Pierre Thomas reflects on King's most famous speech and why his dream still resonates today.
Martin Luther King:	I have a dream that one day…
Pierre Thomas:	Sixty years ago, the hopes and, yes, dreams of the Civil Rights Movement converged in what was truly a historic moment as the pilgrimage of 250,000 people culminated on the National Mall at the feet of the Lincoln Memorial. The country had never seen anything quite like this—a spectacle of consequence involving a

nation grappling with race, freedom, issues of class, and simple human dignity. What would King have to say that day? Would there be violence? How would police react? How would the nation respond? The fact that there were 6,000 National Guardsmen and nearly as many D.C. police mobilized tells you everything you need to know. But why is it that all these years later we pause to remember and ask the young to study that day? What is it? Why are we still drawn? Why can't we let that day go? Why mustn't we let it go? Perhaps it is because what was at stake, because we know right now the journey towards a more perfect union is far from over. But the answer lies in King's speech, undoubtedly one of the most important in the nation's history. Many remember the sweeping, hopeful, spiritual, oratory of what at times seems more like a sermon.

Martin Luther King: I have a dream that one day, on the red hills of Georgia, sons of former slaves and the sons of former slave owners, will be able to sit down together at the table of brotherhood?

Pierre Thomas: But King's words that day were also political, aggressive, piercing, even biting. He was demanding action and indicting the country. The speech begins with a reference to the Emancipation Proclamation, and how it freed slaves, but within forty words, King has this to say—

Martin Luther King: But 100 years later, the Negro still is not free. One hundred years later, the life of the Negro is still sadly crippled by the manacles of segregation and the chains of discrimination.

Pierre Thomas: And later this—

Martin Luther King: We have also come to this hallowed spot to remind America of the fierce urgency of now.

Pierre Thomas: King rose to the moment, spoke to the moment in a speech that inspires us, motivates us, and, yes, haunts us to this very day. For *This Week*, Pierre Thomas, ABC News, Washington.

Martha: Our thanks to our Pierre Thomas for those important reflections.

Part B Henry Kissinger Died at 100

Anchorman: Tonight some late breaking news coming in. Former Secretary of State, renowned diplomat Henry Kissinger has died. He leaves a storied political history, having served

Appendix I Scripts

	multiple presidents, shaping foreign policy for generations. ABC's George Stephanopoulos has more on Kissinger's incredible life and career.
George Stephanopoulos:	For more than sixty years, Dr. Henry Kissinger was one of the most influential and controversial figures in American foreign affairs. The Jewish refugee who fled Nazi Germany in fifteen with his family, Kissinger became a U.S. citizen in 1943, awarded both the Nobel Peace Prize and the Presidential Medal of Freedom. The Republican stalwart served as a part-time Foreign Policy Advisor to both Presidents Kennedy and Johnson as well. In 1969, Kissinger was a political scientist at Harvard University, when President Richard Nixon named him National Security Advisor.
President Richard Nixon:	I shall nominate and send to the Senate for confirmation the name of Dr. Henry Kissinger.
George Stephanopoulos:	Four years later, he became Secretary of State.
Henry Kissinger:	There is no country in the world where it is conceivable that a man of my origins could be standing here next to the president of the United States.
George Stephanopoulos:	Kissinger helped reestablish relations between the U.S. and China, worked to relieve tensions between the U.S. and Soviet Union, which resulted in a nuclear weapons treaty.
Henry Kissinger:	It is a significant step towards the prevention of nuclear war.
George Stephanopoulos:	Back in the U.S., with the Vietnam War becoming increasingly unpopular, Kissinger played a major role in the Nixon administration's policy that escalated then ended the war. Tensions rose when Kissinger helped orchestrate the controversial and secret U.S. bombing campaign in Cambodia, which killed tens of thousands of people. In 1974, the Watergate Scandal led Richard Nixon to resign, but Kissinger stayed under President Gerald Ford. He left office with the Ford administration in 1977, continuing informally advising presidents of both parties. Kissinger was a diplomat until the very end, meeting with leaders around the globe, traveling to China over the summer, meeting with President Xi Jinping in September, seeing Ukraine's

President Zelensky during his trip to the U.S. His presence on the world stage felt long after he officially left. Last year, I sat down with the former Secretary of State as he reflected on his life of service.

George Stephanopoulos: Any key decisions you would take back today?

Henry Kissinger: You know that's a question I'd offer no answer. And I have developed no great answer for it because I've been thinking about these problems all my life. It's my hobby as well as my occupation and so the recommendations I made were the best of which I was then capable of.

George Stephanopoulos: Dr. Henry Kissinger was 100 years old.

Anchorman: Remarkable life of service. George, thank you.

Part C   Queen Elizabeth II Died at 96

Norah O'Donnell: Good evening and thank you for joining us on this historic Thursday night. The world is mourning Queen Elizabeth II, who died this afternoon at the age of 96, surrounded by family at her summer home in Scotland. Earlier in the day, Buckingham Palace announced that Her Majesty who ruled over the Commonwealth for a record of seventy years was placed under medical supervision. Her doctors were concerned about her health. Family rushed to her side. In accordance with the royal line of succession, her oldest son Charles immediately became King, which puts her grandson Prince William next in line to the throne, followed by William's eldest son, nine-year-old Prince George. Just before her death was announced, a double rainbow appeared over Buckingham Palace as a crowd gathered. President Biden visited the British Embassy in Washington late today and left a message in a condolence book. In a statement, he said Queen Elizabeth was a stateswoman of unmatched dignity and constancy, who deepened the bedrock alliance between the United Kingdom and the United States. We have a team of reporters, covering the death of the Queen, described as a stalwart leader and CBS' Charlie D'Agata will start us off from Buckingham Palace. And good evening, Charlie. What's the scene like there?

Charlie D'Agata: Good evening to you, Norah. There's been an outpouring of grief and emotion here at Buckingham Palace. Thousands of people have gathered to pay tribute despite the rain. And although this is a moment that we've all been expecting, it's hard to imagine this country without her. The official notice hung on the gates of Buckingham Palace in accordance with royal protocol. The Queen died peacefully in Balmoral this afternoon. Senior members of the royal family race to be at her bedside today at Balmoral Castle, her summer home in Scotland. Prince Charles now King Charles, was already there. Her grandson Prince William who came without Kate and the Queen's other children made their way to the royal residence. Prince Harry traveled by himself and came later. Megan remained behind in London. On the Queen's death, His Majesty King Charles III issued the statement: "We mourn profoundly the passing of a cherished sovereign and a much loved mother." The new Prime Minister Liz Truss said the country is devastated.

Liz Truss: Queen Elizabeth II was the rock on which modern Britain was built.

Charlie D'Agata: The Queen was last pictured meeting with the Prime Minister on Tuesday and standing on her own smiling by the fire, cane in hand. The 96-year-old monarch was hospitalized last October, suffering from what the Palace called episodic mobility problems, forced to cut back on most public engagements since, only appearing in a few of the events during her platinum jubilee marking seventy years on the throne. She slowed down considerably, appearing more frail in recent weeks for the significant weight loss and the death of Prince Philip in April last year, her husband of more than seventy years, pay reminder that her reign was moving into its final, inevitable chapter. Tonight, the country mourns not just the passing of a national figure, but part of its very identity, the only monarch most have ever known. Now the Queen is expected to remain in Scotland through the weekend before she's brought down here. King Charles will make his first televised address tomorrow and finalize the plans for his mother's funeral. Norah?

Norah O'Donnell: Charlie D'Agata outside Buckingham Palace. Thank you.

Part D Zhang Guimei, a Dedicated People's Teacher

Newscaster: The woman is named Zhang Guimei, who was listed as one of the top ten people that moved China in 2020 by China Central Television and

	a national outstanding member of the Communist Party of China.
Zhang Guimei:	我写入党申请书的时候，我还记得我写了那么一句话："我一定要做焦裕禄式的人。"（I remember on my application form for Party membership, I wrote this line: "I want to be like Jiao Yulu."）
Newscaster:	In 2002, Zhang was a rural teacher. Seeing the backward and unequal distribution of educational resources in China's poor mountainous areas, she vowed to build a free senior high school for girls in the mountains, so to offer them education and a possibility to go to the world beyond the mountains.
Zhang Guimei:	我就想，如果这个女孩子受高等教育，她就能改变三代人的命运。（If a girl receives higher education, she would be able to change the fate of three generations.）
Newscaster:	However, in half a year after she established the school, nine of its seventeen teachers resigned because of the poor conditions. Six out of the eight remaining teachers were Party members.
Zhang Guimei:	八人，六个党员。党员在，阵地就应该在啊。我说"开会！"（Six out of the eight remaining teachers were Party members. Party members should fight till the end. So I convened a meeting.）

Zhang Hongqiong (Teacher of Huaping Senior High School for Girls): 那时我们没有钱，也穷啊，然后她在二楼，就带着我们画了个党旗，然后把誓词写上，然后我们就开始宣誓。（Back then we were on a really tight budget. On the second floor of our school building, she led us to draw a Party flag, and write down the admission oath. Then, we took the oath.）

Zhang Guimei:	我一句，他们一句。我一句，他们一句。我说"我们为共产主义奋斗终生"的时候，后边的声音全是哭声。那种严肃，神圣，那种感觉从来没有过。（I led and they followed. When I said, "Fight for communism for the rest of my life," I couldn't stop crying. That solemnity and sacredness were something that I had never experienced before.）
Newscaster:	From that day on, Zhang Guimei, together with other teachers, as well as the students, went all out.
Zhang Guimei:	读清华北大是我们的一个目标，终极目标，给山里人有一个交代，给山里人一个自信。（Tsinghua University and Peking University were our goals. We wanted to send a message to people in the mountains, and to enhance their confidence.）
Newscaster:	Three years later, all 96 students of the school's first intake were

admitted to universities. Zhang, together with the rest of the teachers, helped 1,804 girls change their fate with knowledge by twelve years of perseverance.

Girl (student of Huaping Senior High School for Girls): 如果没有张校长，像我这样的，孩子都已经三岁了。我觉得是她改变了我的命运。（Without the help of Zhang, I might have been nobody but a mother still in the mountains. It's her that changed my destiny.）

Zhou Yunli (Teacher of Huaping Senior High School for Girls): 可以说是有了张校长，有了女高，我才能有了今日的我。我才能继续读书，上大学。所以我走到女高，用自己所学去帮助那些当时跟我一样家庭困难的孩子．（It's Zhang that founded the girls' school and helped me become who I am today. That's why I was able to get further schooling and enter a university. That's why I came back to the school to use what I have learned to help children in the same situation as me.）

Zhang Guimei: 我这辈子的价值，我救了一代人，不管它是多还是少，毕竟她们后面走得比我好，比我幸福，就足够了。（I helped these girls, no matter how many. That's my contribution of my life. Any way, they will be better off and happier than me. I'm satisfied with it.）

Unit 3　Food

Part A　The Ultimate Chinese Food Tour—Peking Duck in Beijing

Walking through the streets of Beijing, you're immersed in the sights and smells of local cuisine. But one dish is so embedded in the city's DNA that it even bears its name.

Host:　　　　I'd like Peking Duck, please. Thanks.

　　　　　　　Yes, Peking Duck. As early as in Yuan Dynasty (1271–1368), this mouth-watering specialty has been a local favorite and no trip to the capital is complete without a taste.

Host:　　　　This is what I've been waiting. Flour pancake here. This is the Peking Duck that was freshly cut, gonna dip into this sweet and savory sauce we have, next step, cucumbers, and then we have scallions here. Alright, bon appétit. Ah. It's so good. You can taste the meat—it's kind of crunchy on the outside—and then the sauce is sweet, mixes with the cucumbers. It's like a birthday present for your mouth.

　　　　　　　The duck I'm eating now was cooked by Bianyifang. The 600-year-old restaurant uses a closed-oven technique that doesn't utilize an open

	flame. The method is cherished enough to have a spot on China's Intangible Cultural Heritage List. Bai Yongming is the inheritor of the cooking style and has been practicing his craft for 40 years.
Host:	So I just tried the Peking Duck upstairs and now I kind of want to see the background about how it's made.
Bai Yongming:	这个烤鸭吧虽然好吃，但是它制作起来非常复杂。首先，它要用北京填鸭，而且要日龄在39天到41天，分量在六斤到六斤二两。在烤制之前呢，这鸭子还要堵塞、灌汤。（Although the Peking Duck tastes good, the cooking process is quite complex. First, we would use Beijing-local stuffed ducks that are 39 to 41 days old. Each duck weighs between 3 kg and 3.1 kg. Before the roast begins, the duck needs to be stuffed and then we pour soup in it.）
Host:	Okay.
	Ducks are filled with a special soup and hung inside the oven where the heat radiating from the inner walls produces a tender result.
Bai Yongming:	Yes, yes, let's do it.
	While Bianyifang sticks to its tradition of closed-oven roasting, just down the street, Quanjude does things a little differently. Quanjude traces its history back to 1864 during the Qing Dynasty (1644–1911). The restaurant specializes in an open-oven roasting style, where ducks are hung over a flame fueled by wood from fruit trees, giving it a slightly crispy skin without sacrificing taste. Their unique style has also secured a spot on China's Intangible Cultural Heritage List.
Host:	Inside the kitchen, the way they cook the duck here is very different from Bianyifang. It's cooked in the open oven. There's actually wood inside of it, which gives it a slightly smoky taste when you try it, and the skin is slightly crispy, but the same amazing taste.
	I've tried two unique styles of Peking Duck, both using time-honored traditions to produce tasty results. So, whether you choose Bianyifang or Quanjude, the next time you have a Peking Duck craving, you're almost certain to have a meal worth remembering.
Host:	That's good. That's good.

Part B Study Finds Highly Processed Foods Linked to Early Death

Host:	Well, the next time you think about reaching for a bag of chips or some

Appendix I Scripts

pretzels maybe, you might want to think again.

Hostess: A just published study, sorry, is revealing the serious consequences of eating so-called ultra-processed foods. NBC's health reporter Ari Bendix joins us now. Ari, break down the findings, what is "ultra-processed" food?

Ari: Yeah, I would like to think of it as sort of just a technical term for junk food, right? So, that's full with lots of flavorings, additives, not very many whole ingredients. Your hot dogs, sodas, ice cream, all of that. So, this particular study was looking at the risk of early death at eating those foods in a group of their 30s, 40s, 50s, and 60s. What it found was that more than 20%, more than 10% of those early deaths were attributable to ultra-processed foods in 2019. That's likely because they increase your risk of heart disease, cancer, diabetes.

Hostess: 10% of deaths?

Ari: Yeah. It's a considerable amount, yeah.

Host: I just was looking at the stuff we had up on the screen, the video, the list, like, this is the stuff that people eat, right? This processed food is, the ultra-processed food is everywhere in this country. I think it was the *American Journal of Clinical Nutrition* that said these foods make up 75% roughly of the daily calories on average in this country. So, how much should somebody be trying to cut back on these types of foods?

Ari: Yeah, I mean we should be eating these sparingly, if at all. But I think the general recommendation from this study said if you're eating half of your diet from ultra-processed foods, maybe scale that back to about a quarter, less than 23%, they found could prevent about around 20,000 deaths among that cohort in Brazil. So, it's considerable obviously, you know, if you want to have a sweet treat or a salty treat every once in a while, that's good. We should be mindful that eating junk food all the time is just not great for our health.

Hostess: Everything in moderation.

Ari: Absolutely.

Hostess: I say that after eating pizza twice this weekend.

Host: But see what you won't do it today and tomorrow, the day after, the day, it becomes a problem when you...

Ari: Yeah, little changes are helpful.

Hostess: Small changes. Alright. Ari, thanks so much.

Part C Seawater Rice—A Solution for Global Food Security

On September 29, 2019, two days before the 70th anniversary of the founding of the People's Republic of China, the 89-year-old Yuan Longping was awarded the Medal of Republic, the country's highest honor, by President Xi Jinping for his extraordinary contribution to the nation's food security, the development of agricultural science, as well as global food supply.

Yuan Longping: 一粒粮食能救一个国家，也可以绊倒一个国家。(A tiny grain could either save a country or bring it down. The importance of food security should never be underestimated.)

According to the 2019 State of Food Security and Nutrition in the World report, over 820 million people are suffering from hunger, and the world is facing huge challenges in achieving the Sustainable Development Goal of Zero Hunger by 2030. According to the UN's Food and Agriculture Organization, there are four dimensions to food security: physical availability of food; economic and physical access to food; food utilization; stability of the other three dimensions over time. Between 1979 and 2005, China received food aid from the UN World Food Program which benefited over 30 million people nationwide. Starting from 2016, the partnership between China and the World Food Program witnessed a total transformation: China turned from a major aid recipient to a leading aid donor, supporting millions of malnourished people beyond its borders.

The development of science and technology is one of the driving forces behind this change. Yuan Longping is considered a pioneer in the field of food science and technology. He has dedicated himself to the research, application, and promotion of hybrid rice. The super hybrid rice that his team cultivated can yield nearly 18.1 ton per hectare, setting a new world record. Hence, Yuan is regarded as the father of hybrid rice.

Yuan Longping: 这个粮食是国计民生的头等大事。我是学农的，我应该在这方面尽我的努力。我最大的愿望就是这个饭碗要牢牢地掌握在我们中国人自己的手上。(Food security is of paramount importance to the national economy and people's livelihood. As an agronomist, I felt that I should focus on this area. My biggest hope is to make sure that the "rice bowl" is firmly held in our own hands so that we, as a country, could feed ourselves.)

In addition, Yuan is also leading the Saline-Alkali Tolerant Rice Research and Development Center in Qingdao. Saline-Alkali Tolerant Rice, commonly known as seawater rice, is a special type of rice grown in tidal flats and desert areas. China's planting of sea water rice began in 1986. With the continuous efforts of scientists, the cultivation of seawater rice has been successfully promoted to a national level, and by planting seawater rice and adopting soil improvement technologies, the previously barren alkali soil is now largely transformed into arable land. By adopting the latest technology, Yuan's team successfully cultivated and planted seawater rice in five different types of saline soil in China.

The team also brought seawater rice to remote deserts in the Middle East. On July 22, 2018, Yuan's team conducted an experiment in planting seawater rice in desert areas in the Middle East. It is the world's first successful case of planting rice in the desert, a move that offers a solution to the global food security.

Zhang Guodong (Deputy Director of the Saline-Alkali Tolerant Rice R&D Center, Qingdao): 在荒漠里面，从学术意义上讲，它也是一种极端情况下的一种盐碱地。我们的稻谷总共收获了901.5公斤，最高的单产产量平均亩产520公斤左右。（Deserts, in a technical sense, are an extreme case of alkali soil. Our rice harvest totaled 901.5 kilograms, with one type hitting around 7.8 tons per hectare.）

Dr. Aziz Abu El-Ezz (Researcher at Agricultural Research Center, Egypt): I'm surprised, actually, and this intelligence, in my opinion, that they bring a lot of genotypes to evaluate under this. This is a start, a good start.

According to the UN's Food and Agricultural Organization, there are approximately 1 billion hectares of alkali land worldwide.

Zhang Guodong: 我们的目标是在八年内推广1亿亩，把1亿亩盐碱地改造成良田，增产300万公斤粮食，多养活1亿人。（We aim to convert 6.7 million hectares of alkali soil into arable field in China, so that they can produce an extra 3 million kilograms of food which can feed 100 million people more.）

Zhang Hongyu (Professor, Tsinghua University): 如果通过国际合作推广这项（海水稻）技术的话，我以为对解决全球粮食安全问题意义非常重大。包括非洲、中东这样的国家，有地但是水资源匮乏，包括其他的技术在这些地方，可能它的限制因素更多。通过中国人的智慧，在解决这类地方的吃饭问题上做出更大的贡献，也是我们为全球人类命运共同体做出的一份贡献。(If the technology were promoted globally through international collaboration, it would be a significant milestone in our effort to solve the issue of global food security. Countries in Africa and the Middle East have vast arable land, but lack adequate water supply. Many agricultural technologies cannot be applied there. If we can help them with our solutions, we will be doing our part for building a community of shared future for mankind.)

Part D Future Food—The Menu of 2030

Future food, the menu of 2030. The world's population has been increasing faster than food production, even with modern agricultural technology. There will be 9 billion people to feed by 2050. Researchers have been looking at new food sources, tweaking existing ones, and even creating entirely new foods. We examine what could be on our dinner table 20 to 30 years from now.

Critters. A 2013 UN Food and Agricultural Organization report reminds us that there are 1,900 edible insect species out there. That some 2 billion earthlings already regularly consume beetles, butterflies, moths, bees, and locusts. Insects are abundantly available and rich in low-fat protein, fiber, and minerals.

Lab meat. Scientists came up with synthetic meat grown in the lab. As early as 2013, scientists have already cultured ground beef from cows' stem cells. Although that lab patty cost $330,000 dollars to make and tasted quite bland, experts predict it will only take a decade or two for an affordable product that looks, cooks, smells, and tastes like ground beef.

Algae. While it is already used as a biofuel, algae is seen as a solution for the problem of food shortages as it can feed humans and animals alike. Algae is the fastest growing plant on earth and has long been cultivated in Asia. Food experts predict algae farming could become the world's biggest crop industry as it can be grown in both the oceans and in freshwater. It is a good source of vitamins and minerals.

Farmed fish. 3.5 billion humans today depend on the oceans for their primary food source. That figure will double in 20 years. Fortunately, humans are aware of this and have implemented sustainable commercial fishing practices and turned to cultivating fish. Aquaculture is going big with 35 countries producing more farmed fish than fish caught in the wild. A milestone was reached in 2011 when for the first time more fish were farmed than beef, a trend that has continued.

GMO chow. Genetically modified food is nothing new. We first re-engineered the DNA of plants in the 80's to make them disease-resistant. By the 90's, GM foods were commercially available. Several food items we consume—fruits, crops, livestocks, even fish—have undergone some sort of genetic modification. These are generally safe and went through strict standards.

3D printed dishes. Straight from the printer and onto the plate, you will be able to fully customize food shapes, textures, tastes, and forms. You can order online your favorite chocolate bar or snack, and 3D print it with a machine at home. The food you're craving will just be a print away.

Unit 4 Travel

Part A Spain's Tourist Hotspots Facing Housing Crisis

Anchorwoman: Going next to the Spanish island of Ibiza and the soaring cost of a place to live there. In many parts of Spain, rental costs have risen steeply in recent years. But in the tourist hotspot of Ibiza, the rise has been magnified by the influx of foreign visitors. And that's left many locals unable to find affordable accommodation and businesses struggling to find vital staff. As Guy Hedgecoe reports.

Guy Hedgecoe: Ibiza is preparing for the summer tourist season. Its beaches and resorts have long been a magnet for holidaymakers, but its success has helped create a housing crisis. Across the Balearic Islands, rental costs have increased by nearly 20% over the last year alone, and in Ibiza, the increases have been even sharper. There are several reasons for the steep rise in rental costs. Higher interest rates and a higher cost of living have discouraged people from buying property. That, in turn, has led to an increase in demand for rented accommodation, pushing up rental rates.

Guy Hedgecoe: Tourism is also a major factor. Last year, 3.7 million people visited Ibiza and the neighboring island of Formentera. Many stay in flats, pushing up rental prices and keeping locals out of the housing market. Cesar Nebrera is a chef, but although he has work, he's been sleeping in his car for the last three years, something which many workers on the island now resort to.

Cesar Nebrera: Near Ibiza, accommodation is very expensive and it's getting more and more expensive. The cost of renting is completely out

	of kilter with what you earn. When you've been living this long in a car, there comes a moment when you say, "I can't do this anymore. I need a home."
Guy Hedgecoe:	Local activists are demanding that this phenomenon be stopped.
Daniel Granda:	The problem we have is that the island's housing is not being used for the purpose for which it was built; it's being used as a speculative business and for tourism.
Guy Hedgecoe:	This situation is affecting local businesses. The O Beach disco and restaurant is preparing for the high season, but finding staff in Ibiza or from elsewhere is not easy.
George McBlain:	I've already got friends on the island whose rent has doubled in the last year. So, when you are looking at workers coming to the island, it's a massive factor and it's well known. So, I think it will ultimately affect people coming to the island and getting workers to come to Ibiza.
Guy Hedgecoe:	The local authorities say the housing crisis is caused by homeowners who break the law by offering their properties to rent for short periods.
Juan Miguel Costa:	The problem is that you earn much more money renting for days or for weeks than if you rent according to the law, which is at least six months. We have a lot of people who is now renting illegally, offering their properties illegally.
Guy Hedgecoe:	As the high season approaches, the question is whether Ibiza's success as a tourism destination can be sustained when housing is such a problem. Guy Hedgecoe, BBC News, Ibiza.

Part B How "Trashy" Tourism Threatens World-Famous Destinations

Anchorwoman:	Tourism is big business. If we take a look at the numbers, a lot more people are traveling now. There are about 1.4 billion international arrivals a year. That number was only 25 million less than 70 years ago. Tourism can be great for a local economy, but what it leaves in its wake can be, well, trashy.
Alton Byers:	No matter where you go, no matter what remote area, they have the same problems: What do you do with human waste? What do you do with solid waste?

Appendix I Scripts

Anchorwoman: Alton Byers has been visiting Qomolangma every year for the last 40 years and is working to develop waste management strategies in the villages near Qomolangma. Tourists end up producing 4.8 million tons of trash per year, and 14% of that is solid waste. And it's the big sites with the biggest problems. Mount Qomolangma, Machu Picchu, Stonehenge are all struggling with an increase of trash left behind.

Yannick Beaudoin: I think you have to think about it as you're going to someone else's home. What would you do in your own home? And would you do the same thing in someone else's home?

Anchorwoman: The island of Boracay in the Philippines, the base camp at Qomolangma in China, are some of the sites that have had to shut their doors to tourists to take care of the pile-up of trash. But why is the pile-up of trash growing?

Yannick Beaudoin: Tourism is now super accessible. Even 10, 20, 30 years ago, it wasn't necessarily that easy or affordable to just hop on a plane and go somewhere. So now, suddenly, everyone can. And so, I think, in addition to that, when you have a bit more of that disposable society approach, where it's just as easy to get a water bottle and just toss it on the side when you're done.

Anchorwoman: So, what is being done about the trash that continues to pile up at tourist sites around the world?

Alton Byers: The tourist needs to have their awareness increased and they need to do their part. Okay? Lodges need to see that this...and I think they know that this is unsustainable. What's going on, the practice is not sustainable. They need to start developing recycling technologies if they're realistically going to address the problem. So, everybody is a player in this.

Anchorwoman: That includes restaurants and hotels at tourist landmarks.

Yannick Beaudoin: We work a lot at the foundation on circular economy approaches, and part of that is, you know, how do you not just transform the consumption side but also the production side? So, do we need to have the plastic straws and the plastic cups and the disposable everything in our tourist areas, in our hotels, in our, you know, visiting centers?

Anchorwoman: Byers and Beaudoin both tapped into a similar solution to tackle the growing pile of trash at tourist sites around the world, and that is to be more mindful, raise our awareness as tourists, tour companies, accommodation providers, and eliminate trash together as a global community.

Part C Rise of Adventure Tourism

Anchorman: Closer look at extreme tourism. Following the disaster, of course, of that submersible heading to the remains of the Titanic. It is a growing industry, but of course, the lure of adventure is incredibly risky. Blasting off into space, trekking down to the Antarctic, to the depths of the ocean, or the peak of Mount Qomolangma. Visiting the farthest reaches of the planet once thought of as impossible is no longer a moonshot.

Ralph Iantosca: I think inside people really want to explore; they want to know what's out there.

Anchorman: And for certain explorers, the sky is the limit for their extreme adventures and the price tags that come along with them, whether it's commercial space travel or visiting the wreckage of the Titanic. But experts say interest in extreme adventure tourism is booming across the board. Globally, the industry is expanding to over a trillion dollars in 2023.

Stephen Ganyard: We're seeing new technologies that are enabling the kinds of adventures we couldn't imagine even years ago. And people need to understand that there's very little backup and that there is quite a bit of risk.

Anchorman: But for many tourists, the risk is the reward.

Ralph Iantosca: It's unpredictable because it's nature, right? In Antarctica, you could be out kayaking or in a zodiac and you could be very close to whales. Or like when we're in Rwanda and we go to see the gorillas. I love taking groups to see the silverbacks. They're very curious. But it's an animal and you're in its world, so there's a level of risk.

Anchorman: Already this year, 17 people have died or gone missing on Mount Qomolangma. Last December, a rogue wave smashed into a ship returning from Antarctica, killing one person on board. And just

	last week, an American woman lost her leg to a shark bite while scuba diving in the Bahamas. Luxury travel planner Ralph Ian Tosca says adventure tourism is becoming more mainstream but that it's not for everyone.
Ralph Iantosca:	A lot of people want to try something they've never done before. You need to do some soul searching before you do these things.
Anchorman:	And of course, when you're climbing Mount Qomolangma or going to the Titanic, those are extreme and expensive trips. But experts want you to remember that the risk is also there for smaller adventures. People have died parasailing, for example. So, it's important to remember that just because a company exists does not necessarily make it safe. Do your research and really be informed before you make that decision.
Female Guest:	You just talked with a family who—
Anchorman:	Yeah, exactly, just two weeks ago, it's a parasailing accident. And that's one of the things that they have to—they didn't do enough research. They tried to do some research, but they believe that obviously there was more information out there they needed to know.
Female Guest:	You can't just risk your life without—
Male Guest:	You've got to do your homework.

Part D What Happens When You Use Your Mobile Phone in the Largest Resort in the World?

Anchorwoman:	The 5G network in the Universal Studios theme park in China's capital, Beijing, offers an optimal experience for visitors who have high expectations for the technological innovations featured in the multi-billion-dollar amusement park. The theme park is located in Universal Beijing Resort. The resort, currently the largest in scale worldwide, opened to the public in September and has since attracted throngs of enthusiasts. Within a roughly four-square-kilometer area, the 4G and 5G networks can support tens of thousands of phone users in the resort at the same time, with extensive indoor digital systems and microcells set in place to meet demand.
Guo Yu:	In the park, there are many high-end user groups. From our user

	traffic data, the 5G offload ratio has reached almost 50%. The number of 5G users and 5G traffic has reached a very high level. We can meet our users' requirements and guarantee meeting the users' needs during peak times.
Anchorwoman:	Visitors often need to wait in excruciatingly long queues in the park, but with the 5G network in place, they can enjoy watching 4K high-definition videos, livestreaming, playing video games, chatting online, or just browsing TikTok while waiting, as the network can guarantee a rate of 300 to 500 megabytes per second or even higher.
A Tourist:	I use the app to check the real-time waiting time and traffic flow. The waiting time shown on the screen is consistent with the actual waiting time. It's not like it will show 10 minutes on the screen, and when I get there, it turns out to be 20 minutes.
Anchorwoman:	Wireless communication base stations ensure the optimal experience for tourists. As a pilot platform for 5G infrastructure, Universal Beijing Resort has been a pioneer in 5G network coverage, ensuring its visitors have the best experience at the popular tourist attraction.

Unit 5 Fashion

Part A Is Virtual Shopping the Future?

Rachel:	In the future, getting dressed may involve a lot more tech than you ever expected.
Neha Singh (Founder and CEO of OBSESS):	So this is where, you know, you can see, like, it's really photo-realistic quality, even though it's 3D.
Rachel:	I see the fur, like moving. Yeah. First up, Amazon's Echo Look. They call it a style assistant. So, we put it to the test, "Alexa, Alexa, Alexa, take a picture", against an actual stylist.
Man:	I want to see. Oh, my gosh, that's crazy. And then there we go.
Rachel:	Let's do a style check.
Rachel:	Its review takes some time, but when it's done, it ranks which one it likes the best.
Rachel:	According to Alexa, I am supposed to wear the light blue daytime outfit. Oh, they say the color is better for you. The outfit shape works better for you.
Rachel:	Amazon's algorithm doesn't stop at telling you what looks good. It also tries

to sell you clothes, but its suggestions are hit or miss. And while the Echo Look may help you decide between two looks, it can't take into account the nuance of where you're going.

Rachel: But when you hear about the development of all these advanced technologies, do you worry about the future of your job?

Man: For me, I personally don't. I think with, you know, the future of technology and fashion, I think it will benefit, like, production and retail. As a stylist, there's just that, you know, interpersonal communication that you can't replace.

Rachel: Since the emergence of e-commerce how we shop is moving away from stores. Some tech companies are trying to enhance the digital shopping experience by introducing AR and VR.

Rachel: How do you see AR and VR changing the shopping experience?

Neha: We see it changing completely. Like, if you think about e-commerce, every brand and every product essentially looks the same online. That doesn't encapsulate what the brand is about. So, we are building the technology that will enable any brand and retailer to create amazing, immersive, discovery-based shopping experiences. I would say…

Rachel: Is it really that much better than online shopping is currently?

Neha: You have to try it. And with this technology, we are getting closer and closer to the real world, because the real world is three-dimensional. It's all around us. It's not just. So whatever technology, it can get us closer to the real world, like, that's going to be the next thing. Eventually, this will be you, because that's the Holy Grail for fashion. It's like, I want to see how I look in this. Not only do you need a 3D model, but you need the physics built into this model to see how this fabric flows. Like, how it kind of stretches. Yeah. So, all of that like is going is becoming possible. We are not quite there yet.

Rachel: If AR and VR want to change how we shop, digital avatars need to actually look and move like humans. Researchers from the Max Planck Institute for Intelligent Systems created cloth cap, which captures how clothing moves on a digital avatar. It can also estimate how clothing looks on different body types. It'll be years before we're shopping in our bedrooms in AR and VR, but technology is getting smarter, and so might our style.

Part B Style Meets Tech at Guangdong Fashion

Narrator: When technology meets fashion? This year's Runway highlights many brands that have adopted smart fabrics and AI-driven production systems. Versatility, sustainability, and health features are in vogue. Ligongmin is arguably the oldest brand on the Runway, established a century ago.

Zheng Liqiang (General Manager of Ligongmin): We are the only time owned brand in South China, specializing in intimate wear. Besides all cotton products focusing on comfort, we are promoting advanced fabrics, such as women's thermal wear, which helps with blood circulation. For men, we have developed fabrics that reduce the risk of hemorrhoids. Intimate clothing is all about health and we continue to make bold explorations.

Narrator: In the age of e-commerce and influencer marketing, fashion is becoming faster. Staying on trend requires a more agile design and production process. Using industry 4.0 software, big data analysis tracks purchasing in real time and helps factories determine how much to restock and when.

Zheng Liqiang: In the past, production and delivery cycles were based on months, but now they are counted by weeks. We need big data to react quickly, but the key is local sourcing, being able to access all the materials in the same region.

Narrator: Having been dubbed the factory of the world for four decades, China's apparel industry is facing competition from Southeast Asia, where costs are lower. The Ligongmin attributes their increasing sales to patented fabrics and traditional craftsmanship.

Zheng Liqiang: Besides large scale productions, we've also kept this small workshop for high-end customers. Craftsmanship gives clothes their soul, something machines can't do.

Narrator: Chinese heritage was on full display at the Guangdong Fashion Week, with brands combining high-tech fabrics with traditional designs. Meanwhile, e-commerce giants like Alibaba and JD.com brought the latest looks to consumers doorsteps.

Huang Fei (CGTN Reporter): China is actively trying to advance its position in the global fashion and textiles value chain, with the Guangdong Fashion

Week serving as a significant milestone in this effort. Key factors in this initiative include high quality production, low carbon practices, digitization, branding, and globalization. It's all part of a three-year plan unveiled by the Guangzhou government last year, aiming to develop the fashion industry into a 1-trillion-yuan industry by 2024.

Shaodong Chen (General Secretary, Guangdong Association of Fashion and Accessories): Guangdong has the largest fashion sector in China with 29 industry clusters. It has the most complete supply chain. You could say the business end of Chinese fashion is here. The industry must work cohesively to leverage automation and data analysis, and strive to produce high quality, fashionable items with better brand recognition.

Narrator: China's retail apparel market is the largest in the world, and is expected to rack up 300 billion U.S. dollars this year. Analysts argue that new fabrics, innovative designers, and international branding are the main drivers for growth.

Part C Why Milan Leads the Fashion Pack?

Tania: Is there an undisputed fashion capital of the world? New York and Paris each have their own fashion week, but in Milan, the Italians now lead the fashion conversation, says *WSJ* fashion columnist Christina Binkley, who joins us now with all the front row details. Hi, Christina. (Hi, Tonya.) So, Christina, has it been a while since Milan Fashion Week eclipsed Paris?

Christina: I don't recall it ever happening before, to be honest with you. It's been a surprise to me. It's been a surprise to a lot of the Italians, who are really enjoying all the love coming at them right now.

Tania: So, what is setting Milan apart these days?

Christina: You know, I think part of it is we've got a brand that's really setting a lot on fire and carrying a lot of other brands along with it. That's Gucci. But, you know, there's something. The world is feeling a little crazy to everybody right now. It's a little scary. We're talking about terrorism and global warming and the response in Milan, it was kind of interesting, but it's sort of like, you know, swing from the chandeliers, because what else are you going to do? And so fashion turned out to be incredibly fun and beautiful.

Tania: That's fantastic. So, tell us about the show is making the biggest splash

	there. You mentioned Gucci right off the top in your piece.
Christina:	Yeah. Gucci's had an incredible year. They got a new designer last, just a year ago, exactly. Now, Alessandro Michele, he's been doing very strange clothing that has just captured the imaginations of a lot of people. I've called it the poet in residence look. It went a little bit poet in disco look this time. Crazy furs and things like that. But it's a look that's sort of capturing everybody's imagination and spreading out to some other brands. Prada also had a killer show this time. Things have been a little bit sleepy at Prada for the last couple of years, but this was a standout collection.
Tania:	And now what about Dolce and Gabbana? You say they went for princess with a twist.
Christina:	Yeah. And I have to say, when I got the invitation, I hope this can show. I'm gonna actually show you. This is the invitation for the Dolce show. When you open it. Gorgeous. I don't think you can hear that, but it's like a greeting card, and it plays the theme song to the new *Cinderella* movie. And I really thought we were gonna see Mickey Mouse or something. It turned out to be not that at all. It was all about the modern princess. This princess might have a safety pin in her tiara instead of a diamond.
Tania:	I love that.
Christina:	Tough nineties princess, it was super fun.
Tania:	My kind of princess. All right, now, Christina, did the angst that seems to be gripping New York designers over the time span between showing looks and selling them, did that seem to be affecting Milan at all?
Christina:	You know, none of the Milan houses were saying that they were going to change the timing of fashion shows, which is what we heard a lot coming out of New York and London. But that level of anger was there. And as a matter of fact, one of the most stunning shows that we saw really sort of affected me afterwards was from Moschino's designer Jeremy Scott. Again, this is a swinging from the lint chandeliers. He had a set that was like a wrecked palazzo, piled with old antiques and wrecked pianos and chandeliers on the ground. And then, he sent several models down with, they had some sort of smoke machine underneath their sort of tulle gowns that were looking very burned and charred. So, smoke was emanating from these gowns as they went down the Runway. Anna Cleveland, actually, she just killed that Runway. She was twirling and dancing. Really stunning memory.

Tania:	I'm loving these images. Those dresses that look half burned are quite gorgeous, actually. Were there any other designers that stood out for you, Christina?
Christina:	You know, yes, there were. Marni was a strong one. Marni is always, she's a perennial favorite, and that was just another lovely collection, I have to say. These are the fall shows, and this design house is doing something very smart. They had a lot of cotton poplins in a fall show. And the reason is that these clothes are actually going to ship in July and August when we don't really want to look at heavy wool. So, I thought it was very savvy as well as a good looking collection. And I was blown away by Roberto Cavalli, which is designed. This is the second ready-to-wear collection from the new designer, Peter Dundas. His last collection, last September, was an absolute dud. I was not looking forward to what we were going to see. He actually did this stunningly beautiful collection. Very long, lean silhouettes, a lot of velvet, all kinds of selvage. It reminded me of Jethro Tully.
Tania:	Uh-huh. Gorgeous!
Christina:	It was beautiful.
Tania:	Gorgeous clothes, all of these clothes! Christina signed me up for one of those burnt ball gowns. I love it.
Christina:	There you go.
Tania:	Thank you so much for that.
Christina:	My pleasure.

Part D Becoming Her Chinese Women's Fashion Evolution in the Past 70 Years

When the People's Republic of China was founded in 1949, the key word was "work". As for clothes…, we love the "Blazy", a type of Russian style dress. Puffy short sleeves, frilled hem, and diverse partners…The Blazy brought out our young woman's passion and beauty. More importantly, the style wasn't as restraining as the Qipao, allowing us greater flexibility in the workplace.

Jumping to the 1960s, the military uniform was the only fashionable style at the time. Back then, the military was his icon to all of us. It was our dream to own a set of military uniform, even if we weren't recruited. There's nothing wrong with those colors of green; the lack of variety makes things a bit monotonous.

In the 1970s…As we all know, began the Reform and Opening-Up Policy! The green-dominated trend finally came to an end. It was a time for us to re-embrace fashion. "Diqueliang" was our favorite fashion darling at that time. It was made of polyester resistant to creasing, diverse in pattern, but it wasn't comfortable at all. However, at a time when ready-made clothes were hard to find, we all loved such material. And with the curly hair, I could be the most fashionable girl in the neighborhood.

In the 1980s, television sets entered many households. TV stars could serve the fashion trends of the day. Besides actors and singers, news anchors were also icons for professional women. Career-minded, women took a liking to the suit as padded shoulders and tight skirts. During that decades, women began demonstrating not only refined taste in clothing, but also independence and confidence.

As for the Golden Age of fashion in China, people today still talk about the fashion of the 1990s with nostalgia and admiration. Oversized suits and jackets, light-colored denim coat and jeans, tight and sexy dresses…and the pager on the belt. The pervasiveness of Hong Kong's pop culture, spread by their films, TV shows, and music, created a fashion boom at a time.

While entering the new century, the Chinese economies rising. And "fashion" turned into a kind of mix-and-match, in a disastrous way…K-pop went viral in China at this time, bringing in exaggerated hairstyles, usually dyed wild curls, dangled decadently in front of the eyes. The past ten years…well, you're quite familiar with that. More and more fashion brands have come here…

Contemporary fashion is characterized by diversity. Instead of talking about fashion, now talk about style. For the Chinese girls today, fashion, or style, is more about being yourself.

Unit 6 Lifestyle

Part A Lie down for a While at an Urban Oasis in Shanghai

Zhang Hong: Here we are at the lunch break slope for office workers in Xuhui District. What makes it particularly popular is its ergonomic design, which makes it an ideal spot for a quick nap. You might think I'm a bit crazy to be here at noon when it's already 26 degrees Celsius. But I heard it's so popular that finding a spot was almost impossible a few weeks ago. It's like lying down on a large deck chair with the pleasant scent of grass surrounding you. It's nice! The idea is known as the 20-minute nature effect. Spending just 20 minutes in a natural setting can significantly refresh one's mind and body.

[Some interviews in Chinese]

Interviewee 1: My job requires a lot of concentration, making me exhausted. Coming here to bask in the sun during lunchtime is perfect.

Interviewee 2: There're not many places like this where you can lie down in Shanghai. If I want to take a nap during lunch break in the office, I can only rest my head on the desk. This ergonomic slope is much more comfortable and allows me to better enjoy nature.

Interviewee 3: There are many dining options here. After playing the basketball, I can have lunch, get relaxed in the sun. It gives me a good mood.

Interviewee 4: The weather has been good recently, and it might not last long. So, I want to grab the chance to spend more time outdoors.

Zhang Hong: This public space has been around for about seven years. However, recent social media posts have made it particularly popular among nearby office workers.

Zhang Dou: We are trying to build a focus area down below so people around that can kind of look over to the activities in the sunken plaza. So, on the north side and the south side, we have benches. For this side, we decided to make it a little different, make it softer and greener. The angle is about 135 degrees—that's something we have tested many times in our office, trying to find a comfortable slope for people to lie down.

Zhang Hong: This slope is part of the Xuhui Runway Park. The over 14-hectare slide used to be a runway for Longhua Airport, which was Shanghai's only civilian airport until 1949.

Zhang Dou: Xuhui River from…It has a lot of high-density development. And I think they were smart when they were doing the master plan for this area. They have planned a riverfront park right along Huangpu River. And then, when you go inside for a few blocks, they also planned this runway park, kind of in the middle of those high towers, so you can take a break from all those tall buildings.

Zhang Hong: Zhang Hong ICS from CGTN, Shanghai.

Part B Living off the Grid

Coy Wire: …right? But for some, there's still an appeal and trying to live off the grid. That means completely self-sufficient, gathering your own food, shelter, power, and water. It's not an easy way to live but it is much simpler and those who do it are saying that it can be tremendously rewarding. Let's travel to the Wales countryside where some people are choosing to live off the grid.

Will Cooke (Brithdir Mawr Resident): We're not saying all of this modern stuff and like all machinery is bad and all modern ways of doing things are bad. We're trying to integrate ancient ways of doing things with modern ways of doing things.

Correspondent: Many of us might try to live more sustainably to help the environment. But some take a more drastic approach, aiming to become self-sufficient like these people living off the grid in the Wales countryside.

Cooke: Brithdir Mawr is an intentional community which has currently got 23 people living on site of ages ranging between two and mid-60s. Started in 1994. I'll take you on a little look around this way.

Correspondent: Intentional communities, eco-villages, housing cooperatives. There are many different types of these communities around the world and they can be traced back to the U.S. and U.K. in the 1940s, inspired by the Back-to-the-Land Movement and popularized by hippies in the 60s and 70s. Two key elements that define Brithdir Mawr's way of living are being off the grid and the community structure.

Cooke: When we talk about the grid, we mean the mains—electricity grid, water, sewage, and waste disposal. We're not part of any of those networks. But that doesn't mean we're completely cut off from society. We're about 80% to 90% self-sufficient on food. Our water comes from spring on the mountain. Heating and cooking is done with wood, harvested from the land. Electricity comes from solar panels, hydroelectric and a wind turbine. Here're some goats. We milk the goats twice a day. We're also making lots of cheese.

Jess (Long-Term Volunteer): So, we're going to be going up to the coppice and starting on that.

Correspondent: Roughly 100,000 people are living in similar ways around the world, according to a 2020 estimate from the Executive Director of the Foundation for Intentional Communities.

Correspondent: And the number has been rising in recent years.

Cooke: We are a non-hierarchical community, so there's no individual in charge. We make our decisions by consensus. We want to have this balance where we're putting more time and energy into working on the land here and becoming more self-sufficient as opposed to putting all of our time into earning money, working for someone else, and then spending that money on the things that we need to live like food. On average, people work one to two days a week, doing other work, because we are paying rent here. There are challenges here but then there are huge challenges in terms of what people are going through in their everyday life out there. And anyone could learn the land skills. Anyone could learn the decision-making process. Anyone could choose to live in a way where you're making being in harmony with the land, being in harmony with the other people around you the priority. There are many, many ways in which people could live, which would give more to the world than they're taking from the world. This is just an example of it.

Part C   A Hygge Way to Happiness

Mary H.K. Choi: Look up "hygge" on Instagram and you'll find 1.7 million posts on woolly socks and hot chocolate. Pinterest experienced a 285% spike on hygge pins, and, last year, it was shortlisted as the Oxford dictionary word of the year. What was once a Danish custom is now big in the U.S. Meik Wiking is the founder of the Happiness Research Institute and the author of *The Little Book of Hygge*, a bestseller that was reprinted three times before its release and is published in 26 countries. Alright, Meik, tell me what is hygge?

Meik Wiking: Hygge is being consciously cozy, but it has also been described as the art of creating a nice atmosphere. It's been called the pursuit of everyday happiness. It's also been called socializing for introverts.

Mary H.K. Choi: Okay!

Meik Wiking: But it's about being together with the people you love. It's about relaxation. It's about indulgence. It's about good food. It's about gratitude. It's about equality. All of those things mixed together is hygge.

Mary H.K. Choi: Would you characterize hygge as a lifestyle trend or as self-help?

Meik Wiking: Actually, neither. I mean, to us Danes, hygge is part of our culture. It's part of our national DNA, perhaps the same way that Americans see freedom as inherently American.

Mary H.K. Choi: If you think hygge just sounds like a trendy Scandinavian catch-all for all the things humans like in the dead of winter—comfort foods and ambiance—you're not wrong. But the Danes' conviction is singular. They burn more candles than anyone in Europe and they eat a lot of candy per capita, all in pursuit of hygge.

Meik Wiking: I think there is, you know, savoring pleasures. Indulgence is, I think, key in terms of hygge, and perhaps also something sinful. I think also hygge is taking a break from demands of healthy eating, so it is about cake, it is about candy, it is about, you know, hot chocolate, it is about alcohol; some even might say it's about, you know, sinful pleasures.

Mary H.K. Choi: Hygge is horrible for your health, conceivably?

Meik Wiking: You could say that. I mean, compared to the Swedes and the Norwegians, we have a shorter life expectancy. We do eat more unhealthy.

Mary H.K. Choi: But Type II diabetes and fire hazards aren't what Danes are known for. They're known for happiness. Denmark consistently places first in the UN's World Happiness Report, an international poll where citizens are asked to self-evaluate on their well-being. The U.S., for all our "life, liberty, and the pursuit of happiness" has never cracked the top ten.

Mary H.K. Choi: So, what does America have to learn from Denmark in terms of happiness and hygge?

Meik Wiking: I think, in many ways, Denmark is what the U.S. would look like if Bernie Sanders was President. I think the most defining feature of Danish culture and life and politics is our democratic socialism. Universal health care, equal opportunities for men and women, free university education, social security. At a certain point, additional income, it does not lead to improved quality of life.

Mary H.K. Choi: Hygge's been huge all over Europe for a while, but it's zeitgeisting nicely stateside. With the help of Danish transplants like Claus

Meyer, a chef and restaurateur, hygge is finding its place in America. Meyer has been living in the U.S. for a year and a half and has hygge over dinner every night with his wife Christina, an interior designer, and their daughters.

Mary H.K. Choi: So, what about this is hygge versus just, like, any other family just eating a meal?

Claus Meyer: We actually have made an active decision not to be on the phone while we are together. And that everybody's included in the conversation.

Viola Filippa Meyer: And I've been to other families where they just don't even eat together. But maybe the parents are doing something else, or they're on their phones or computers, and they don't really talk to each other. And I can we really feel the difference in the atmosphere.

Mary H.K. Choi: While Meyer does impart some Danish culture to his staff, offering paid maternity and paternity leave, he doesn't think Denmark runs a monopoly on hygge. It's that naming it and recognizing it gives it power.

Mary H.K. Choi: Do you fear that, you know, doing hygge will fade the more time you spend here?

Claus Meyer: It could, probably. In many, many years. But it is one element of life. I naturally believe that many people find that moment, they just call it something else. Some moment of groundedness and where you're close to other people and listen with your heart and see people with your heart. And even though we're more conscious about it, I can't imagine that it doesn't exist somewhere else.

Part D The Magic of Bookshops

Li Wenrui: "Every bookshop is a condensed version of the world," says Jorge Carrión, a Spanish writer and literary critic who roams the globe in his study of unique bookshops. Having traveled to over 1,000 bookstores, Carrión has put all his anecdotes and meditations into the recent work *Bookshop: A Reader's History*. As it has been translated into Chinese, the writer came to Beijing this May to chat with Chinese literati and visit some of the local bookstores. In his interview with *China Daily*, Carrión reiterates the role of traditional bookshops in the post-digital era, which reminds us of the magic of the written word.

Li Wenrui: Welcome Mr. Carrión, and thank you for being with us today. First, I want to congratulate you on your first Chinese version of your book.

Jorge Carrión: Thank you very much!

Li Wenrui: The first question is how many bookstores have you visited so far? Do you keep a record?

Jorge Carrión: I don't really know, but definitely more than one thousand, for sure.

Li Wenrui: You collect cards from every bookshop?

Jorge Carrión: I collect cards, I collect like ugh...notes, bookmarks, also photos. I've got thousands of photos of the best, the most interesting, the most beautiful bookshops on the five continents, yeah.

Li Wenrui: You have been to China before, and plus this time. So, do you have any suggestions for Chinese bookshops to help them not only survive but also thrive in the future?

Jorge Carrión: I was in China only once before 15 years ago. And I hardly recognize Beijing. I think, the city has changed a lot. And now, the new bookshops in Beijing are very similar to the most important bookshops around the world, especially in Europe and in America. They are following the same international trends. And I think that it is good. But I think they cannot forget the tradition and the particular aspects of the Chinese traditional bookshop.

Li Wenrui: Do you have any particular bookshop that you like?

Jorge Carrión: I really think that Kid's Republic could be the most beautiful children's bookshop I have ever visited. It's amazing: the design of the space and the selection of books for children. And I also really like Page One in the center of the city. Because it is very original and interesting that the bookshop is open 24 hours of the day—the day and the night. This is not common. And also the design and the architecture of the building is interesting and unique. Because in Page One, you are like in six different bookshops inside the same bookshop. And I think this kind of experience is really beautiful and nice. For me, I'm someone that is always thinking the space where there is a relationship between the reader and the book. I find these bookshops really the beginning of a new way to understand how the bookshop can bring you completely different experiences.

Unit 7 Sports

Part A Health Benefits of Exercising Outdoors

Lara: All right, turning now to the warmer weather. We are looking at why taking your fitness routine outside might be more beneficial than working out indoors. It's a story we first saw in *The Washington Post*. Rhiannon Ally is in Central Park doing just that. Good morning to you, Rhiannon.

Rhiannon Ally: Hey, good morning, Lara. Yes, it is a gorgeous morning here in New York City. And millions of Americans, spring is finally showing its face everywhere you look. It is so beautiful out here. And we're talking green exercise this morning. And green exercise means exactly what you think. It's taking your exercise routine and moving it out into nature. And a review of 10 different studies looking at about 300 people found that there are big benefits. We're talking mental and physical benefits. It can help with your motivation. It can help with your willingness to stick to a routine. It can also just help you to work out even harder. In fact, in all of these studies of all the things they measured, indoor exercise did not trump outdoor exercise in any of the areas, Lara. So, it seems the research is pretty clear on this.

Lara: I mean, looking at you makes me want to just get out there and do it. I can see how it would work. But what do researchers think it is?

Rhiannon Ally: So, we've all heard the saying, I'm gonna go take a walk and clear my head or perhaps a lot of us have even said that ourselves. It turns out, there is something to that. When you get out into nature, it really forces you to put your worries aside, at least for the time being, to stop stressing so much, to really reset your brain. And that means afterwards, you can concentrate better. You can just do all things better than you could before that. And that's on top of the benefits we already know about, Lara. We're talking increased blood flow to and oxygen to your brain.

Lara: All right, but there are some caveats. It's not just as simple as getting out there, right?

Rhiannon Ally: So, there's always an exception, right? This is mainly for people who live or work in big cities or spend a lot of time there. We love looking at those big skyscrapers. They're beautiful. But when you're talking about pounding the pavement, if you want those mental health benefits, you're not gonna get the same benefits if you're running in a city-urban area versus if you get out into a forest or a park, or even a beach. Just immersing yourself in mother nature is where you're really gonna get those benefits. But you don't have to start out with these long, strenuous workouts. You want to work your way up to that. So, you want to talk to your doctor or perhaps your personal trainer. Set some small goals and then work your way up to that. And Lara, I know how much you love tennis. So, I'm hoping today you can get out on the tennis court and play a game. I'm gonna go get my kids. We're gonna go for a walk in the park. I can't wait. Spring is finally here.

Lara: Oh, you got that right. I will be on the court. And I cannot wait to get out there. I'm so glad the weather is finally cooperating. And hey, great workout for the cameraman, too. Give her some applause. Everybody getting their outdoor, green workout on.

Part B Five-year Runner on How the Sport Transformed His Life

Amy Robach: Now to a man making history in a sport we both know and love. We recently had the opportunity to meet up with former professional soccer player Hellah Sidibe. Not only has he been running every day for 1,851 days straight, but he's also the first black man to run all the way across America.

T. J. Holmes: Yeah, we caught up with him, caught up with Hellah. He shares, of course, our deep love of running. He takes it to another level, of course. But he's telling us how he started running. And it completely transformed his life. Check this out.

Amy Robach: So you're going to run, you said, how many miles tonight?

Hellah Sidibe: I'm going to do three to five.

T. J. Holmes: You're an ultra runner now.

Hellah Sidibe: Yes.

T. J. Holmes: And you hated running until what age?

Hellah Sidibe: Until 2017, five years ago. And that came about because I wanted to hold myself accountable and face my fear of running. Running is just a byproduct of soccer. When it comes to get on the line, you messed up, and you run for two hours, it's a—it was a punishment. It really was. So you start having this fear and phobia about running.

Amy Robach:	Of running.
Hellah Sidibe:	I wanted to start it two weeks ago just 10 minutes a day. And within a week, I fell in love with it. So I ran to my fiancé. I said, "Hey, I think I want to do this for the rest of my life." I've been going every day since May 15th of 2017. I haven't missed a day. And I've covered 14,375 miles in that time. And with that, I ran across America from L.A. to New York City, 84 days, 3,061 miles, 14 states, and 36 miles a day.
Amy Robach:	Did you just say 36 miles a day?
Hellah Sidibe:	Yeah, 36 miles a day.
Amy Robach:	We love your story.
Hellah Sidibe:	Thank you.
Amy Robach:	Take us back to the beginning.
Hellah Sidibe:	I was born in West Africa. Mali is one of the poorest countries in the world. Most people make less than $ 1 a day. Even though you're poor, everybody looks out for each other. And you have no idea how poor you are. And I came to the U.S. based on education. My parents were both doctoral degree students.
T. J. Holmes:	You said things weren't going your way. How bad off did you get in your personal life?
Hellah Sidibe:	Yes.
T. J. Holmes:	And did running end up ultimately saving you?
Hellah Sidibe:	I moved to Seattle at the time. And as a professional soccer player, I didn't have food to eat. So, when I was going through a tough time, I said, "You remember that one time you thought this was it? You just have to smile because you'll eventually get over it. Eventually it all subsides." And then running made me find that joy again. Running made me feel invincible. When you're out there putting miles in, when you just feel like you're on top of the world, you can do anything you put your mind to.
Amy Robach:	Hellah, I have to tell you, you are speaking my language. Because I have said running had gotten me through some of the lowest, toughest points in my life. It's the only thing that, when you're feeling weak in every other way, you can feel strong, even it's just completing one mile.
Hellah Sidibe:	I'm not going to give up on it. I'm not going to give up on life, because it will make me that much stronger. You know that Kelly Clarkson,

"What doesn't kill you makes you stronger."

Kelly Clarkson: What doesn't kill you makes you stronger.

Amy Robach: Well, I ran to that song.

Hellah Sidibe: Plays in the back of my head. Because it doesn't kill you, it will make you stronger.

Hellah Sidibe: It's been 163 days since I've been running. And my goal is to go for 365 days.

T. J. Holmes: How is the—you said your fiancé started—you two—

Hellah Sidibe: Yeah, so when I started this journey, it was a self exploration. And she told me, "Hellah, we should put this on YouTube." People were asking me, "Are you still running every day? Can you update?" So I started doing updates. That's when we were introduced to the public. And we became YouTubers. I just shared my journey with them to let them know that it is possible. If I can do it, you too can do it.

Amy Robach: Running is intimidating to a lot of people. They'll say, "Oh, I can't run as fast".

Hellah Sidibe: Yes.

Amy Robach: But you were talking about it's the effort, not the time.

Hellah Sidibe: Yes, effort, not the time. A 12-minute mile and a 6-minute mile are still a mile. If you're able to run 30 seconds and you've got to walk for 5 minutes, you are still a runner. So you just got to be, you know what, I'm grateful my body gave me this today. And that's how it is. And I'm going to move on.

Amy Robach: Also, on your list of things to do is the New York City Marathon 2022.

Hellah Sidibe: Yeah, we should run it together. I think that'd be so dope.

Amy Robach: I'm in.

Hellah Sidibe: Are we doing it? Are you in?

T. J. Holmes: Let me get back to you.

Amy Robach: Oh, but I happen to have inside information. It's something you did yesterday.

T. J. Holmes: I did not know that was at the end of this piece. Yes, it is official, I have signed up for the New York City Marathon.

Amy Robach: Yes.

T. J. Holmes: It is official. I have a receipt. But Hellah was great. We did run a little bit with him that day as well. And so we will see him at the marathon. But he's just a great spirit. We loved the time with him.

Amy Robach: Yeah, it was amazing. We loved him. We also want to thank our friends at Hudson River Park for letting us run, on camera, the path we run almost every day. So, thank you.

Part C VR Sports

Azuz: New digital technology is changing the way people perceive sports that have been strictly analog for centuries. This is being done with the aid of virtual reality, sights and sounds that are completely computer generated, and augmented reality overlays of computer images on actual physical environments. It's not for everyone. For one thing, there's something called cyber sickness, which is like motion sickness. Experts say that when you perceive movement on a screen or a VR headset, but your body isn't actually moving. The confusion this creates in the brain can make you feel disoriented and sick. Some health experts are also concerned about the excessive amount of screen time that many people already get. Do electronic images need to be added even at the gym where many go to unplug in the first place? For supporters of the new technology, it can add excitement and opportunity for a new type of workout. But a membership at $200 per month at Black Box VR costs several times that of other gyms.

(Begin video clip)

Kristie Lu Stout (CNN Correspondent): I'm at Ski Tech, an indoor training center for winter sports in Hong Kong, trying out this ski simulator. Sensors track my motion. Software recreates snow conditions and the panoramic screen transports me to snowy mountains. There's no snow in Hong Kong, but thanks to virtual reality, I can hit the slopes and fine tune my skiing technique, and for some entrepreneurs, virtual and augmented realities define the next generation of fitness and sports. San Francisco's Market Street, home of streetcars, and tweets and now a virtual reality gym. At Black Box VR, opened in 2019, your body transforms into a controller and real-world exercises are flashy attacks in the virtual battleground.

Unidentified Male: Woo. All right. I feel like I'm blowing up.

Preston Lewis (Co-founder of Black Box VR): Black Box VR is the world's first, resistance-based virtual reality gym.

Stout: Now, walk me through the Black Box VR experience. You go to a Black Box VR center. You walk into a private booth. You put on the VR headset and then what happens?

Lewis: So, you—you go in like you said. You put that headset on, and you are immersed in this vast of epic, futuristic sporting arena, and the crowd's cheering for you and chanting for you. You actually have a—what we call a dynamic resistance machine, that is massed to the virtually reality space. You start to do chest press, shoulder press, back row, all these different compound fitness movements, and as you're doing those movements, you're actually shooting a fire beam or an ice shard and creating these epic attacks against your opponent.

Stout: For Preston Lewis, co-founder of Black Box VR, fitness is all fun and games. He says the gamification aspects of the experience are designed to make people addicted to their workouts.

(Crosstalk)

Stout: Let's talk more about VR, because you said that virtual reality is a great way to trick people into committing to a fitness routine. What do you mean by that?

Lewis: Absolutely. Yes, and most people have a super hard time sticking to their fitness routine. With virtual reality, it's the exact opposite. Video games have been created by some of the world's best behavioral psychologists and they just have it down. They have this perfect little timing, the perfect little dopamine drips and achievement or award.

Unidentified Female: It's really hard to stop moving once the game gets going. So the mix of technology, the game itself, everything intertwines, keeping you moving and it's keeping you from getting distracted from the workout itself.

Stout: At Black Box, members work out in their own private room where is the resistance machine that pairs the VR headset. Lewis says that for users working out in the world of Black Box, 30 minutes

Lewis:	feel like 10. When you're working out in the game, do you feel the passage of time? You know, and that—that's one of the great things about virtual reality as well is time dilation. When you're on a treadmill, you're—you're sitting there, you're—you're time walking or you're running and jogging and you look at, you're like OK, it's been a half hour, and then you look at the clock and it's been like five seconds. You know, and so, it's the opposite with VR. I'm very tech-forward and I think applying virtual reality game in workouts. Super awesome concept, ready player one. So really want to try it out.
Stout:	Black Box is currently only available in gyms across the U.S., but Lewis says the company is hoping to expand internationally.

Part D Dragon Boat Festival—A Blend of Tradition and Competition

Laura Westberg:	The rhythmic beat signals the start of the Dragon Boat Festival where people traditionally eat rice dumplings and paddlers flock to the ocean to take part in races. It dates back to the story of the patriotic poet Qu Yuan over 2,000 years ago. He drowned in a river and the legend goes that people raced out in their boats to try and save him and threw balls of sticky rice into the river to protect his body from being eaten by fish. The festival is well known. There is also a cultural element to it.
Law Hon Cheung:	In Chinese medicine, we observe the patterns and changes in nature. And then, we try to incorporate the observations to explain like what happens in human body. Dragon Boat Festival is dated on like fifth day of the fifth month of the Chinese Calendar. Many regions actually enter the rainy season. This temperature is actually favorable to the growth and activity of many pests.
Laura Westberg:	Historically, people fought against these threats by using pungent herbs tied into pouches or hung on doors, which some still do to this day. Those herbs are wormwood, calamus, and Chinese mint, and are sometimes used to decorate traditional dragon boats.
Law Hon Cheung:	It's believed to have an effect of repelling the bad lucks. So, they would want that on their dragon boat.

Laura Westberg:	The herbs are also used as ingredients in medicines for treating ailments prevalent at this time of year.
Law Hon Cheung:	Duanwu Jie is, actually, the meaning of it is the start of summer. Seeing this humid climate when this like extra moisture occur in our body, we call it dampness. We can use this herb to clear this dampness from our body.
Laura Westberg:	Wormwood is used to treat digestive issues, calamus is used for the hotness in stomach, and Chinese mint, which is a cooling effect, can be used to treat flu.
Laura Westberg:	Back on the beach, paddlers are getting a last training session in before the upcoming race. Some hope a pouch of herbs could help turn the tide in their favor come race day.
Chris Barnes:	If somebody gave that to a hundred percent, we definitely love to incorporate that. It's not something we've done before. But, who knows? You know, maybe that would be the thing that gave us the action, made us win the races. Yeah.
Laura Westberg:	For many, this festival is about tradition. But for those out in the water, the focus is on the competition, Laura Westberg, CGTN, Hong Kong.

Unit 8   Entertainment

Part A   Wordle—The Daily Obsession of Millions

Anchor:	Throughout the morning, our Susan Spencer is all about fun and games. First up, word play. For millions of Americans, morning means breakfast, coffee and—most importantly—Wordle.
Susan Spencer:	I mean, my Wordle is usually done in the first 10 minutes of consciousness.
Everdeen Mason:	Yeah, I mean, some people, they play our puzzles the minute they come out.
Susan Spencer:	Everdeen Mason is the editorial director of *The New York Times'* Games.
Zoe Bell:	This has a good amount of space, though, in between.
Susan Spencer:	Zoe Bell is its executive producer. What do people think when you tell them what you do for a living?

Appendix I   Scripts

Zoe Bell:	It is a cocktail party winner.
Susan Spencer:	Wordle, the brainchild of software engineer Josh Wardle, was acquired by *The New York Times* in 2022. A year later, it was played 4.8 billion times.
Zoe Bell:	Tens of millions of people are playing it every day.
Susan Spencer:	OK, let's see what happens. Absolutely nothing, that's the worst possible result. If you're late to the game, here's how it works: Each day, there's a five-letter mystery word. You get six chances to figure it out. With each guess, you'll learn if your letters are wrong, right, or right but in the wrong spot. Can you put your finger on what it is in the design of Wordle that accounts for this astonishing success?
Zoe Bell:	If you think about what happens with every guess in Wordle is you get new information and I think that's really compelling. And then when you solve it, there's a really, really big moment of satisfaction.
Susan Spencer:	Tell me about it. [Laughs] Well, it depends on how soon you solve it.
Everdeen Mason:	It might be a lot of other things too, or is it a better strategy to…
Susan Spencer:	OK, so what's the foolproof strategy for doing that?
Everdeen Mason:	You know, some people have the same word every single day.
Susan Spencer:	Is that a good idea?
Everdeen Mason:	It can be, I mean, especially if you pick one with a lot of vowels.
Susan Spencer:	ADIEU is the most popular first guess—all those vowels—but here's depressing news: Statistically, ADIEU does not yield the best results.
Zoe Bell:	I actually think that the starting word is important, but so is the second word. Because if you have a good starting word and then you blow it by not eliminating other letters in your second guess, then you're gonna be at five or six (tries).
Susan Spencer:	But this is the genius of its design.
Zoe Bell:	Right, yes.
Susan Spencer:	—a genius that's made Wordle a national phenomenon—"All we have is one lousy T."—at breakfast tables everywhere.

Part B   Conservation Group Fighting to Save Marilyn Monroe's Los Angeles Home

Anchor:	That's Marilyn Monroe in the 1953 comedy film *Gentlemen Prefer Blondes*. Today, more than seven decades after that iconic

	performance, there's a new drama surrounding the only home the Hollywood star ever owned. Here's CBS' Carter Evans.
Man:	One of the most famous stars in Hollywood history is dead at 36.
Carter Evans:	Marilyn Monroe's death in 1962 shocked and saddened the world, and many consider the Brentwood home where she died, one of the last links to her legacy.
Jeff Zarrinnam:	We have a lot of history here that needs to be preserved.
Carter Evans:	Jeff Zarrinnam is on a mission to save famous L.A. landmarks.
Jeff Zarrinnam:	This is the place you want to see the Hollywood sign from.
Carter Evans:	—and he knows where all of Hollywood's hidden gems are, like Marilyn Monroe's handprints at the Chinese Theater. This is about as close to Marilyn Monroe as most people will ever get.
Jeff Zarrinnam:	Well, she also has a Walk of Frame Star.
Carter Evans:	All just a few miles away from the Spanish style bungalow she owned and loved. The home is hidden pretty well from the street outside, and it's been more than 60 years since Monroe died here. The house has changed hands several times over the years, but this is the first time its owner wants to tear it all down. The L.A. city council is supposed to vote later this summer to determine if the eight-million-dollar property should be labeled as a landmark, but the home's owners don't like the spotlight, and they're suing the city for the right to raze it, saying the tourist attraction is a nuisance to the neighborhood.
Adrian Scott Fine:	We want to see meaningful preservation and protection honoring Marilyn Monroe and the place in which she lived and loved.
Carter Evans:	Adrian Scott Fine is President of the Los Angeles Conservancy, which works to preserve culturally significant structures. Like the historic Angels Flight Railway and the Cinerama Dome theater. One possibility with Marilyn's house:
Adrian Scott Fine:	—to relocate it in a place where it makes sense.
Carter Evans:	The Star Line bus we're on already makes regular stops at some of L.A.'s more visible famous homes. Recognize this one?
Jeff Zarrinnam:	This is the house. Can you believe that?
Carter Evans:	There are homes like this that you grew up watching all over this town.

Jeff Zarrinnam:	All over the place.
Carter Evans:	But since you can't see Marilyn's home from the street, Zarrinnam thinks moving it might just be the best solution.
Jeff Zarrinnam:	But then you gotta find a site for it.
Carter Evans:	All this left us hungry for a visit to one of Hollywood's most recognizable pieces of real estate.
Jeff Zarrinnam:	Here we go.
Carter Evans:	Alright. Pink's has been in the same spot for 84 years.
Shop Owner:	Our family likes to call ourselves the little hot dog stand that could.
Carter Evans:	It's so iconic. The city of L.A renamed the intersection here Pink's Square. So while the fate of Marilyn's home is unclear, this building's going nowhere.
Shop Owner:	This building is here, permanent for sure.
Carter Evans:	—to be relished by fans for years to come, Carter Evans, CBS news, Hollywood.

Part C Pop-up Exhibition in Hong Kong Marks 50 Years of Bruce Lee's Death

Anne Cheng:	When people think of kung fu, Bruce Lee is the name that comes to mind. But more than just his moves, he is also known as a cultural icon for his style, films, and philosophy. With a career spanning across Hong Kong and the United States, Lee is credited for helping to bridge the gap between the East and the West. And to commemorate 50 years since his passing, the Hong Kong Heritage Museum has organized "Bruce Lee: A Timeless Classic", a pop-up exhibition that lasts till January. Here are magazine covers that focus on Lee's Jeet Kune Do, a type of martial arts that he founded and draws from various types of combat disciplines and philosophy. Another highlight is commemorative calendar for the premiere of his film *The Way of the Dragon*, which was his only completed directorial film. Visitors can also get a chance to check out action figures, stamp collections, comics, and a replica of Lee's diagrams on different ways to attack.
Brian Lam:	In our pop-up display, you can see that we mainly focus on Bruce Lee's legacy on popular culture. We put more efforts on the ambiance in the display gallery, so we tried to feature Bruce

	Lee's teachings. We have a mural wall that features his wording and his legacy about how he dealt with the challenge, overcome the difficulties and also how he encouraged himself to be a more confident and stronger person to prepare for future challenges.
Anne Cheng:	Many of you may know this iconic laugh from Bruce Lee's last film *The Game of Death*. But you may not know that this film didn't just inspire fashion choices and other films like *Kill Bill*, it also inspired the format for many video games. Its original concept involves fighting your way to the top of the tower by defeating enemies on each level, sounds familiar?
	And for those wanting a wider glimpse into Lee's life and achievements, a bigger and permanent exhibition is offered on another floor. For example, you can find Lee's notes on a fight choreography from *The Game of Death*, which was completed by another director and standing actors after his death.
	These were boxing and fencing masks worn by Lee. On top of Wing Chun, he also incorporated elements from those sports into his Jeet Kune Do. And you may not have guessed this, but Lee liked to write poems in his free time.
	To mark this anniversary, the museum has also organized a Bruce Lee-themed camp for children, and hosted a screening for *The Kid*— a film in which Lee debuted at nine years old and co-stared with his father. He was discovered by director Fung Fung, whose daughter also co-stared with him in the film.
Alice Feng So Bo:	In observing Bruce Lee's every move from their interactions, my father detected that he had a lot of personality, so this script was tailor-made for him let him shine in his own element. During filming, my dad really gave him free rein to move about and express himself in his own way. And the cameras would cater to his movements.
Anne Cheng:	Outside the museum, a snapshot with Bruce Lee's signature move is usually a must.
Milk Hui:	In 1978, I watched *The Game of Death* with my family, and I became his fan up till now. To us, he's hero. He's so powerful especially for boys who need to find idols to model after. He's number one.
Man 1:	I remember when I was a kid, I used to watch his films, and it really

Appendix I Scripts

	inspired me to join like kung fu lessons, tae kwon do, karate. At that time, there's a lot of people interested in doing that, so it was great for everyone to get healthy. So it's a pity that he's gone, I couldn't believe it the day he passed away. So, yeah, it gives me a lot of memories.
Anne Cheng:	Even though Bruce Lee passed away at such an early age, his legacy certainly continues to have a lasting impact on the world. Anne Cheng, CGTN, Hong Kong.

Part D Will Unique Popcorn Buckets Bring People Back into Movie Theaters?

Anchor:	With the drop in numbers of the box office, movie studios are turning to some unique methods to try and get people back into the theaters. As Leigh Waldman reports 2024 could turn into the war of the popcorn buckets.
Leigh Waldman:	Summer movies are struggling to make waves.
Paul Dergarabedian:	The box office is down at this point about 24% versus last year.
Leigh Waldman:	Memorial Day weekend, a traditional major money maker for the film industry, saw the lowest box office in 29 years. Last year, writers and actors' strikes mean we can expect a lighter than usual slate of movies this summer. Further driving fears of a theatrical meltdown.
Paul Dergarabedian:	So we need a hero right now for the box office.
Leigh Waldman:	That hero could come in a very strange form. Ryan Reynolds teasing the upcoming *Deadpool* and *Wolverine* by declaring the war of the popcorn buckets. Media analyst Paul Dergarabedian says movie theater chains are looking for any angle to compete with streaming.
Paul Dergarabedian:	There are so many ways that movie theaters are trying to get people to come to the theater. Great food and beverage, reclining seats, great sound and vision.
Leigh Waldman:	Now they're enticing customers with collectible concession vessels for major releases like *Taylor Swift's Eras Tour*, *Ghostbusters: Frozen Empire*, and *Dune: Part Two*, which achieved viral infamy for its bizarre bucket design, including a lurid lampooning on *SNL*. That film went on to an eighty-two and a half million-

dollar opening weekend. Dergarabedian says that proves all fair in movie marketing.

Paul Dergarabedian: That's the biggest opening weekend of the year so far for *Dune: Two*. I think that proved that the popcorn bucket just created a conversation and built a brand even bigger.

Leigh Waldman: In New York, I'm Leigh Waldman.

Unit 9   Business

Part A   The Collapse of the Silicon Valley Bank

Coy Wire: ...with the collapse of a bank in the United States over the weekend that has people worried about losing their money and businesses on the verge of going under.

Silicon Valley Bank, an epicenter for tech start-up companies with $175 billion in deposits at the end of 2022, has collapsed. One reason, those rapidly rising interest rates we've been talking so much about on this show.

Well, they made the Treasuries, in which the bank had invested money, less valuable. So, the bank started to sell them at a loss, and that scared people who had money there. So, they went on what's called a bank run, withdrawing all their money in a panic. The more people that did that, the more others wanted to do the same. Inevitably, the bank collapsed.

The FDIC, or Federal Deposit Insurance Corporation, seized control of the bank, and President Biden said yesterday that all depositors would get their money back. And businesses that kept assets there, well, they would have money to pay their employees.

The collapse of Silicon Valley Bank had a ripple effect on a second bank. The same sort of bank run hit Signature Bank shortly after. It had its doors slammed shut, as regulators warned that keeping it open could threaten the entire financial system's stability.

Now, there are fears that other banks may be next. There's a term for this sort of spread of fear over people losing money when banks collapse. It's called contagion. So yesterday morning, President Biden addressed the nation for the first time publicly to try to ease those fears, knowing that the panic could cause a devastating economic fallout for people and businesses around the world.

Joe Biden: All customers who had deposits in these banks can rest assured, I want them to rest assured, they'll be protected, and they'll have access to their money as of today. That includes small businesses across the country that bank there and need to make payroll, pay their bills, and stay open for business.

No losses will be—and this is an important point—no losses will be borne by the taxpayers. Let me repeat that. No losses will be borne by the taxpayers. Instead, the money will come from the fees that banks pay into the deposit insurance fund.

Because of the actions of that—because of the actions that our regulators already taken, every American should feel confident that their deposits will be there if and when they need them. Second, the management of these banks will be fired if the bank is taken over by FDIC; the people running the bank should not work there anymore.

Third, investors in the banks will not be protected. They knowingly took a risk, and when the risk didn't pay off, investors lose their money. That's how capitalism works.

And fourth, there are important questions of how these banks got into the circumstance in the first place. We must get the full accounting of what happened and why those responsible can be held accountable.

Part B How Much Income Is Needed to Buy a Home?

Coy Wire: We start today talking about the current housing market in the United States. The dream of buying a home in America is becoming more expensive. High mortgage rates, rising home prices, and low home inventory are pushing home ownership further out of reach for first-time buyers. A new bank rate analysis says Americans wanting to buy a medium-priced home need to make at least $110,000 a year. That's almost a 50% increase in the last four years. This changes the calculation for potential homebuyers who are torn between buying or renting a home. Here's Redfin.com's chief economist, Daryl Fairweather, with more.

Daryl Fairweather: Right now, it is more affordable to rent than it is to pay for a mortgage. And historically, that hasn't been true. But if the mortgage payment that you would have to pay is less than 30% of your monthly income, then that means that you can afford that mortgage pretty comfortably. How long are you going to stay in the home? If it's for more than five years, there is a good chance that you will build enough equity such that when you go to sell your home, you will make a return on your investment. But if you sell too soon, you might end up losing money. So, it's a risk and a reward. We're expecting this next year to be a bit better for buyers than it was last year. That's because mortgage rates have started to fall and also more listings of homes are coming on the market, which means there are more options for buyers.

We are forecasting a slight correction in prices this year, down 1%. But it's just not enough to really make it or break it for a homebuyer. It's probably going to keep getting less affordable, unfortunately.

There's a trade-off that a lot of young people have where the places where they can earn the most money are the places that have the most expensive housing. So, I think it's completely valid to say, like, I want to live in New York City, for example, and I'm going to have access to all these jobs that are going to improve my career prospects. And then one day when I am more established in my career, I'm going to say, move to a suburb where it's more affordable and I'm going to be a homeowner that focus on your entire life and not just like reaching this one goal that isn't as attainable as it used to be.

Part C   Chinese Vehicle Manufacturer BYD Unveils New Double-Decker Bus Design

...the iconic red double-decker bus, transporting London's passengers since the 1920s. For the last decade, older models have slowly been swapped for electric versions, to meet clean air targets. But London has one of the biggest bus networks in the world, so there is demand for more electric buses to join the fleet. The Chinese firm BYD is a major player in this market, supplying electric buses and partnership with Alexander Denis since 2013. Now it's launched its own up graded double-decker. The key selling point, greater battery power.

"Uniquely, this bus is the first example of us using our new blade battery in a commercial vehicle and what that brings with it is advantages of safety, performance, and value for money." The bus has a range of up to 400 miles from a single charge, making it ideal for London's lengthy bus routes. "So we can see here that what's really unique is that the battery is being used as a structural component within the vehicle." BYD says its design allows for more space for passengers and better temperature control for the capital's varied climate. "For the end user, nothing looks any different. They see a red bus, but they're getting all the benefit of this technology." The vehicle also has a tight turning circle, handy for navigating London's narrow streets and heavy traffic. "As you can see, the inside of this bus looks pretty much like your traditional London double-decker. But developers are hoping that its modern design is going to help contribute to London's clean air." London already has lower emissions than many other major cities and several manufacturers contribute to the array of electric, hybrid, and diesel buses. "London has, you know, really high ambitions for the bus network to become zero emission by 2030, and that's going to be a hell of a lot of work. So, really our work starts now. But we have a great foundation with which to push on."

BYD hopes its new double-decker bus design will move from the test track to providing a passenger service by the end of this year, though the details of any deal with Transport for London have yet to be announced.

Part D Stock Trading Halted After Markets Plunge at Market Open

This is an NBC News Special Report. Here's Savannah Guthrie.

And good morning, everybody. We're coming on the air with breaking news. This is the New York Stock Exchange. The trading day is just beginning on Wall Street. And there are fears that the Dow will drop and drop quickly. And we're already seeing that futures over the weekend were down so much that they actually had to put an emergency trigger that stopped trading. And the expectation and fear is that we will see markets in freefall this morning here in the U.S. as they have done in the global markets already today. Let's get right to CNBC's Becky quick, who is at the stock exchange for us. Becky, this is expected but here we go. The numbers are already in freefall.

That's right. Savannah, this morning, we had been looking at the futures down by 5%. As you mentioned, that's limit Dow, that as far as they will allow the futures to trade down before the opening bell. But in the very first moments of trading here, you're seeing the stock market move well below that right now. It looks like the Dow is down by about 6.9%. This is some massive pressure. If you haven't looked at 401K over the last couple of weeks, I wouldn't recommend doing it today. Because just over the last two weeks, we had already seen the markets down by about 12%. A little more than that. Now, you're adding declines of more than 7% today. Now, the 7% that we're sitting at right now, that would kick in additional circuit breakers. If we get to these levels, the new circuit breakers are there to try and prevent panic selling which is what you might be looking at right now.

The circuit breakers kicks it, kick in when, Becky?

For the S&P, the S&P 500, the circuit breaker would kick in down 7%. If we are looking at down 7% for the S&P 500, you will see a pause in trading for 15 minutes. Then, if you see the S&P trading down 13% from those original levels where it closed on Friday, it would pause again for another 15 minutes. And then if you see a 20% decline at any point before 3:25 p.m., because the markets closed at 4 p.m. If you see a decline of 20%, the market would actually halt trading for the day. Now it's worth pointing out that we have not seen these circuit breakers triggered since they went into effect in 2013. At least not at these levels. We'll be watching this very closely because you're sitting near those levels right now. I'm looking at the S&P right now down buoyed by 6.95%. So, we are near those levels where you would see some circuit breakers kick in.

The big reason for this, obviously, people concerned about coronavirus and what that is going to mean for the broader economy. If you look at within the stock market, the sectors that are really getting hit the hardest. You have to look at the travel industry. Cruise lines in particular, I saw some of them trading down 10% to 12% this morning. Airlines have been watching them trading down 4% to 7%. And then if you're looking at hotels, a lot of pressure on those things too.

The other big issue, Savannah, is that we really saw a big issue with the oil markets over the weekend, too. If you're looking at crude oil this morning, it's been down more than 20%. Crude oil alone. And that's having a huge impact on all of the oil companies out there, big oil companies, including Exxon Mobil and Chevron as well. This is happening not only because of concerns about an economic slowdown, but also because the Saudis and the Russians really got into a big fight over the weekend. And they are…Saudis are really trying to do an oil price war here. And that's why you're seeing all of these issues kind of come to a head this morning.

And the timing couldn't be worse to be having that kind of turf war at the very moment that the global economy is really struggling under the weight of the coronavirus. But stick there, Becky, if you will, we're gonna keep an eye on the Dow Jones as what we're showing already right there. So, we're talking about those that are circuit breakers that was in regard to the S&P index. The one we're showing you is the Dow, but in any event, you get a sense of it. And here, all the U.S. markets as they open this morning.

Unit 10   Technology

Part A   A Legal Loophole of Driverless Cars

The Anchorman: Also tonight, more and more communities are test driving autonomous cars. But in California, a legal loophole lets driverless vehicles avoid any penalties for traffic violations. Bigad Shaban from our Bay Area NBC station investigates.

Bigad Shaban: Driverless cars have run red lights, crashed into other vehicles, even swerved into wet cement and other construction zones. Plus these so-called Robotaxis can't exactly take orders from police.

Witness of the Car Accident: Sir, there's no one there.

Bigad Shaban: So, when traffic laws are broken and there's no one behind the wheel, who gets the ticket? In Texas and

Appendix I Scripts

	Arizona, where driverless cars are now common in some neighborhoods, companies that own the vehicles can be fined. But not in California! Even when driverless cars break the rules of the road, we've learned there's not much law enforcement can do. Here in California, traffic tickets can only be written if there's an actual driver. So no human, no fine.
Michael Stevenson (California Attorney):	We are very much in the wild west of the legal grey area when it comes to driverless cars.
Bigad Shaban:	California attorney Michael Stevenson has been representing car accident victims for more than a decade. Laws are going to have to change.
Michael Stevenson:	Right. Absolutely are. (What) we really need is an overhaul, a new set of laws for driverless cars.
Bigad Shaban:	It was August when California regulators gave the green light for GM's Cruise and Google's sister company Waymo to expand and start collecting fares as they shuttle passengers across San Francisco. But just two months later, the California DMV determined Cruise posed an unreasonable risk to public safety. Cruise saying the most important thing for us right now is to take steps to rebuild public trust, even if it means doing things that are not uncomfortable or difficult. The company pulled all 400 of its driverless cars in the U.S. off the road. Cruise declined our interview request, but we did hitch a ride with its main competitor, Waymo, which is now the only driverless fleet in America actively picking up passengers.
Chris Ludwick (Head of the Product Management for Waymo):	Not all autonomous vehicle technologies are equal.
Bigad Shaban:	Chris Ludwick heads product management for Waymo. If driverless cars can still make mistakes, what makes you so convinced they're still safe enough to be on the road?
Chris Ludwick:	Well, there have been examples pointed out where driverless cars continue to need to improve. When we make an improvement at once, that's fixed in our system and the whole fleet gets better. And so the technology is

	only getting better from here and it's already really good.
Bigad Shaban:	Waymo and Cruise say their own researchers found their driverless cars are in some ways safer than human drivers. Neither company has experienced a single death. Waymo has traveled more than 7 million miles. Cruise, more than 5 million. But some question if that's enough of a track record, since human drivers on average cause 1 death about every 100 million miles.

Irina Raiku (From Santa Clara University): I think all of us are still struggling to understand whether they really are safer than human drivers, and in what ways and in what ways they might not be.

Bigad Shaban:	Irina Raiku has the Internet ethics program at Santa Clara University, and says we humans have been forced onto a sort of test course for driverless cars. Other drivers, pedestrians, cyclists are, all of a sudden, now guinea pigs.
Irina Raiku:	Absolutely. All of us really, who live in areas where such cars are driving.
Bigad Shaban:	Meanwhile, California's DMV says it is working to update regulations, so the next stop for these driverless cars could be new rules and more accountability. Bigad Shaban, NBC News, San Francisco.

Part B Are "Digital Humans" the Wave of the Future with AI?

Wire:	Pop quiz, hot shot. In which decade was the term "artificial intelligence" used for the first time? The 1950s, the 60s, the 70s, or the 80s? If you said 1950s, ding, ding, ding. Dartmouth Professor John McCarthy is credited with coining the term with three other researchers at a summer workshop in 1956.

Some 68 years after the term "artificial intelligence" was not much more than a vague concept, AI, as we know, is popping up in our daily lives, everything from schools to the workplace, to the freaking, freaking, freaking—to the club. That's right, virtual DJs.

And CNN spent the day with a British start-up that makes what they call AI-integrated digital humans, including a DJ that performs at shows around the world. And we wanted to show you all this new idea because we want to hear from you.

Let us know what you think. Are these advancements a good thing, simply fun and harmless? Or as some believe, are they hurting us in the long run and taking away jobs from real life humans?

Woman: Combining 3D technology from the world of gaming with voice cloning and motion capture, Liverpool-based start-up Sum Vivas are now creating digital human avatars integrated with artificial intelligence.

Dex (DJ and Influencer, Sum Viuas): Hi. Hello, everyone. I am Dex, the U.K.'s first AI-integrated digital human.

Dennis Harris (Co-founder and CCO of Sum Vivas): In the performance space, it's game changing. The DJ that I manage, Dex, last—in the last two weeks has performed in New York, Paris, and Milan. We're creating new music. So we're actually working with record labels. We are working with promoters on shows. We're working with brands now to do influencer-type brand collaborations.

Rob Sims (Co-founder and CCO of Sum Vivas): Utilizing digital humans integrated with AI helps to bridge the gap between technology and people. They're available 24-7, 365. They don't take holidays. They have the ability to be multilingual and they learn and remember every conversation.

Woman: But should we be worried about AI's integration into the world of work?

Jennifer Ding (Senior Researcher of the Alan Turing Institute): We do see the dreams that have taken over the headlines the past year. The generative AIs, the chatbots, the LLMs, all kinds of applications are emerging. But alongside, I think there is this fear of skills replacement. So when we rely on automated tools, what skills are we losing in the process?

Rob Sims: AI is absolutely not scary. It is part of our future. We're moving to a stage where digital humans will start to become just another member of the team with added benefits for that team and obviously the customers they serve.

Part C How Artificial Intelligence Changes Consumers' Lives?

Stephen Hawking: I believe that the rise of powerful AI will be either the best thing or the worst ever to happen to humanity.

Anchorwoman: Artificial intelligence has enabled computers to hear, see, think and learn. We'll show you how AI technology is changing our lives by creating virtual personal assistants, visual search engines, and even cashier-free supermarkets.

Anchorman: The AI industry is experiencing a period of rapid growth, from traditional manufacturing to strategic emerging industries. Many international, domestic companies are making attempts to grab a share of the fast-growing market. iFLYTEK is one of the companies that manage to become a leader in voice recognition amid Chinese market.

Jiang Tao (SVP of iFLYTEK): Since being launched after seven years of development, iFLYTEK has become the largest OpenAI platform in the domestic market. Take robotics, a recent hot spot, as an example, there are more than 10 thousand robotics developers on our platform. Actually, most of the robots you see today use iFLYTEK voice interaction capabilities. The AI voice technology developed by iFLYTEK has been used in multiple areas such as education, healthcare, home, offices, transportation, and media.

Qu Lingna (Personnel of iFLYTEK): This is one of our most popular products, EasyTrans, translation machine. Now, let's have a try!

The Translation Machine's Voice: Today the weather is good. And the outdoor temperature is about ten degrees below zero.

Anchorman: While continuing to push forward in R&D in AI voice, iFLYTEK is also cooperating with other businesses to launch new products, to expand the market. For example, the smart sound system launched by iFLYTEK in collaboration with JD.com adopted microphone array in far-field voice recognition which makes it possible to realize voice wake-up within a range of five to eight meters.

Liu Hui (Customer of iFLYTEK): The one thing on exhibition that impressed me the most is the smartphone. In the future, we don't need to have so many controllers. Instead, we can control all kinds of appliances with voice. The application of iFLYTEK AI system in healthcare also shows great potential.

Lin Bo (Marketing Manager of iFLYTEK): In the past, it might take an experienced doctor five minutes to analyze an X-ray. But now it takes just one second for our AI system to go over 200 X-rays. Therefore, the system can assist the doctor with some fundamental work. Therefore, making the decision-making process more efficient and quicker.

Anchorman: According to the development plan of the new generation of

	AI launched by the State Council, by 2030 China is expected to increase the size of the AI industry to more than one trillion RMB, driving the development of related industries to more than 10 trillion RMB. iFLYTEK earn revenue of 2.102 billion RMB in the first half of the 2017, a year-on-year growth of 43.8%, showing that AI is generating huge economic value in the tech industry.
Jiang Tao:	The product is not a replacement of the existing healthcare system. Instead, it is a complementation. Besides, AI is also able to constantly help existing industrial change through providing valuable data based on its machine-learning capabilities.

Part D China's AI: Competition or Cooperation?

I'm Robert Lawrence Kuhn and here's what I'm watching: Artificial intelligence, AI, developing rapidly in China.

AI is heralded as transformational for humankind; some say AI will disrupt industries and societies, even alter powers among nations. Conceived in literature and philosophy, AI was founded as a field in the late 1950s in the U.S.

One of AI's founders, the late Marvin Minsky of MIT, a friend, told me how the founders saw the right vision, though they were overly optimistic in their forecasts. Ray Kurzweil, whom I also know, famously celebrates "the singularity", when non-biological intelligences vastly exceed human intelligence.

Conversely, some scientists fear that AI could literally take over the world, with uncertain, even dire, consequences for humanity. While the United States continues to dominate AI, China's ambition is to become a leader in AI.

In 2017, China's State Council issued its guideline, the Next Generation Artificial Intelligence Development Plan, envisioning China as a global innovation center by 2030.

Why has China made AI a national priority? Which AI areas and industries are targeted? What are China's competitive advantages, disadvantages?

Some say AI has become a kind of battleground between China and the U.S. Six factors drive China's AI strategy: a robust data ecosystem, adoption in traditional industries, creation of new industries, specialized talent, education and training systems, and ethical and legal consensus.

In developing AI, China has advantages of recruiting national resources, huge user base, mega-project velocity, and the world's second largest economy. The U.S. has advantages of first mover, top universities, diversity of researchers, venture capital ecosystem, openness, and transparency.

All seek breakthroughs in big data intelligence, deep machine learning, brain-like computing, multimedia computing, human-machine hybrid intelligence, swarm intelligence, expert systems, even quantum intelligent computing.

AI has hit its tipping point; it cannot be stopped. AI will be a major driver of industrial upgrading, consumer marketing, healthcare, education, smart cities, public security, agriculture, and of course national defense. At the same time, AI raises complex ethical, legal, social, and security questions, from threatening human jobs and privacy to empowering autonomous war machines.

So, why should AI be a win-lose competition? Perhaps, it's not so much China versus the U.S., but humans versus machines? Shouldn't China and the U.S. be partners, not adversaries, to assure that AI serves humanity, not the reverse? I'm keeping watch. I'm Robert Lawrence Kuhn.

Unit 11 Literature

Part A The "Dan Brown" of Chinese Literature Makes U.S. Debut

Zafar Anjum: Here's a thrilling story about a Chinese thriller writer who critics are calling the "Dan Brown" of Chinese literature. Five million copies sold in Chinese, but Western publishers just weren't interested, at least for a while. *WSJ*'s Anna Russell joins us now to explain how it all ended happily, and happy ending is always good with it, with a, with a thriller, isn't it? Tell us some… Tell us more about this author, Mai Jia.

Anna Russell: Mai Jia is a huge author in China. His books have sold over five million copies, altogether.

Zafar Anjum: five million! I'm told that only 1% of books are more than 5,000 copies. So, five million is a heck of a lot.

Anna Russell: Yes, he's a superstar in China. He's won some of their biggest literary awards, and three out of four of his novels have been made into a television series or a film or both.

Zafar Anjum: Now, his typical, his thrillers, don't follow the typical, you know, the typical sort of formulaic thriller writing thing. How do they work?

Anna Russell: Right! So, it's not a traditional Western spy thriller. It's slow moving. It's an in-depth character study. There's a lot of psychological portraits, and

	it's kind of dense, very literary prose. It's, it's more in the way of Jorge Luis Borges than Dan Brown, actually.
Zafar Anjum:	But, but, but just as, just as spectacularly successful. Now there's a chicken and egg problem here for Western publishers, and Western publishers don't often speak Chinese or read it, which is the more important thing. So, how do you get a phenomenally successful book in China that's written in Chinese to a Western publisher and get them to buy it?
Anna Russell:	So, it's very difficult for a contemporary Chinese novel to actually get published in the U.S. or the U.K. in English, mainly because it's difficult for the Chinese author to pay for the whole translation themselves before they can be sure of a publishing deal, because usually the publisher will pay for the translation once they've decided to make the deal. But it's kind of a chicken or egg, because, you know, they can't afford to make the translation until they have a guarantee of the deal.
Zafar Anjum:	Okay, Mai Jia's been heralded as a literary phenomenon. Thank you very much.

Part B What If Robert J. Sawyer Writes a Sci-fi Book About China?

Reporter:	This man has arguably the greatest claim to be "Canada's godfather of science fiction." This man also won both Hugo and Nebula Awards, and he is Robert J. Sawyer.
Robert:	You know how he's famous: They had actually on *Star Trek* recently; they had a starship named "Liu Cixin".
Reporter:	Is there a possibility that Hai Ya could form a new Chinese influence in the world of science fiction?
Robert:	I think absolutely. The most important thing that has to happen now for Chinese science fiction is for Liu Cixin not to be a one-off. We need more of that, so this year's winner and next year's in subsequent years winners. When a Chinese author is even just nominated, let alone winning, nominated for the Hugo Award, it tells the worldwide science fiction community that this is something to pay attention to. So, this is a breaking down of walls that's long overdue, and I'm delighted to see it.
	The kind of science fiction that I write and Cixin Liu writes, um, Liu Cixin, is what we call "hard science fiction". That is not in the ascendency in the

West. Here in China, however, there is still a lot of vigor and strength to hard science fiction. China has been encouraging science fiction clubs on university campuses and it's been encouraging the inclusion of science fiction works in the curricula in various topics, because it's recognized here that the reading of science fiction is almost a prerequisite for a career in science and technology. And so, yes, absolutely science fiction is in decline in the West because science and technological supremacy is in decline in the West, and it's in the ascendancy here in the East.

Reporter: You mentioned that you have been to the China Dinosaur Museum and you're also interested in dinosaurs.

Robert: Yes, very much so.

Reporter: I wonder if you know that in Zigong City in Sichuan Province, we actually have the best dinosaur museum in the world.

Robert: I know. I have not been to it yet.

Reporter: And it also the one of the best places where you can get to see the fossils.

Robert: Absolutely yes. It's wonderful to come to China. I've come now six times, six, and there are so many things I want to see in China. I want to see the Three Gorges Dam. I want to see so many things. I want to see the Terracotta Warriors, and of course, I want to see the great dinosaur museum. My friend Kim Stanley Robinson, very famous for *Red Mars*, Green Mars, Blue Mars, and other books, says science fiction is just history continued. If you don't have a lot of history, it's very hard to write about the far future. I think here in China, if I were writing a novel inspired by or set in China, that I would probably be inclined to write much farther in the future, as my friend Cixin Liu often does.

Do not try to copy Western science fiction styles, voices, themes. Tell your own stories. What Cixin Liu proves to the world is that a story deeply rooted in Chinese culture can find an audience worldwide. Don't try to pretend to be Western writers; be proud and loud Eastern voices.

Part C Tanzania's Abdulrazak Gurnah Wins 2021 Nobel Prize for Literature

Rhys: It began as a typical Thursday for Abdulrazak Gurnah, but by lunchtime he'd gone down in literary history. The 72-year-old Tanzanian being named the winner of the Nobel Prize for Literature. Getting the news on the phone in his kitchen in Canterbury, England.

Appendix I Scripts

Gurnah: And this man says, "Hello, I'm from the Swedish Academy, congratulations! You have won the Nobel Prize for Literature" and I said, is this a prank?

Rhys: Shortly afterwards, the rest of the world knew as well.

Mats Malm: The Nobel Prize in Literature for 2021 is awarded to the novelist Abdulrazak Gurnah, born in Zanzibar, active in England, for his uncompromising and compassionate penetration of the effects of colonialism and the fates of the refugee in the gulf between cultures and continents.

Gurnah: Some people walked; many drowned.

Rhys: Gurnah is the first black African to win the Nobel Prize in Literature since 1986. He fled Zanzibar after an uprising in 1964. As citizens of Arab heritage like himself suffered persecution, Gurnah arrived in England as an 18-year-old, going on to write 10 novels. His work has explored the continuing effects of colonialism on Africa and given a voice to the experience of refugees.

Gurnah: There is a kind of meanness I think, in this response to people who want to come from elsewhere to Europe. It's not like they're coming empty-handed or anything like that; it's not like they're coming, saying "Here's my begging ball, please fill it."

Rhys: The Swedish Academy has promised to become less Western-centric as well as less male-oriented. Gurnah's win follows two female prize winners in 2019 and 2020. His books including *Afterlives* and the Booker shortlisted *Paradise* were written as he worked as a professor at the University of Kent. Demand for them could now go through the roof.

Meron: We don't have any more clue than anyone else who's going to win, and then when it's announced, people are excited and want to buy the books. There's often a shortage, so we have to be ready to order them in, as soon as the announcement is made.

Rhys: Gurnah's win breaks ground for African writing, although he's still in a small minority of non-Western literature laureates. The Swedish Academy has faced questions over the prevalence of Europeans and Americans in its previous choices and over the relevance of this 120-year-old prize in today's world. The sudden fame that has fallen on Abdulrazak Gurnah in becoming the 2021 Nobel laureate in literature answers both of those questions for this year, at least. Paul Rhys, Al Jazeera, Stockholm.

Part D University Launches Taylor Swift-Inspired Literature Course

Bradley: She's a pop and country music icon. Taylor Swift has enchanted people all over the world with the music we know all too well. And guess what Swift fans, there's a new title on the way; it's not a song or an album. It's called Literature (Taylor's Version), and it's believed to be the first Taylor Swift-inspired literature course in Europe. Say hello to its lecturer Ellie McCausland. So, we'll kick off by talking about the Taylor Swift songs and we'll, sort of say, you know, okay: What is this song about? Why is it interesting: What kind of techniques is she using? And you know, I'll make a little mind map on the board. I love a mind map and we will use that discussion as a basis to then tease out the themes and the issues that are present in the literary text. Swift's songs are often inspired by English literature classics with themes that you might find in *Jane Eyre*, *Romeo and Juliet*, and *Alice in Wonderland*, but do people really know the writer behind this particular *Love Song*, "Romeo, take me somewhere I can be alone"?

Bradley: Literacy courses, would you actually go to UNI if you knew it was inspired by Taylor Swift?

Student A: Probably, because it makes me go more to do that.

Bradley: Are you a huge Swift fan?

Student A: Yeah, yeah, to be fair, give us a pleasure.

Bradley: I mean it is the perfect love story, isn't it?

Student A: Yeah!

Bradley: I'm gonna read a little line here to you: "Romeo, take me somewhere we can be alone." Who do you think wrote that?

Students B: Hmm, thinking, Taylor Swift.

Students C: I'd have to agree.

Bradley: How would you feel if your English literature course was inspired by the Taylor Swift?

Students C: I think I'd be a bit lost because I don't really know about many of the songs. I know the radio hits and the classics, but that's about it.

Bradley: You could probably shake it off, though.

Students C: Yeah…

Bradley: Awful. I don't think they'll shake that moment off, but can this new Swift-inspired literature course pull it off? You might find me there in the Autumn to find that. Bradley Harris, Five News.

Appendix I Scripts

Unit 12 Nature

Part A Fire Season in Australia

Coy Wire: Experts worry that the combination of El Nino and the underlying global heating spells a summer of extreme heat and fire. Australia suffered its worst fires in 2019 and 2020, burning millions of acres, including homes and natural habitats. The fire season down under usually starts in October and ends around March. It's a dangerous, sometimes deadly time for people and wildlife. Already this year, bushfires have hit parts of the country and firefighters are working hard to keep up with the help of volunteer crews. There are tens of thousands of volunteer firefighters across Australia, especially in rural areas. We're about to join two of them now.

Lauren Wilson (Advance Firefighter): When I tell people I'm a firefighter, I actually get a lot of mixed reactions. Oh, you do all that for free? What makes you do that? It really does spark a lot of curiosity in people.

Coy Wire: Australia battles some of the largest and hottest wildfires on the planet. The fire season in Australia typically runs from October until the end of March, when temperatures are at their highest. Most of the firefighting is conducted by the Rural Fire Service, a volunteer force separate to state emergency services. The New South Wales Rural Fire Service has more than 70,000 members.

Andrew Hain (Senior Deputy Captain, Picton Rural Fire Brigade Internal Flight Planner): We were founded in 1939 by local farmers and local residents that needed a firefighting service in the area, and it was a bunch of guys with old trucks or trailers. Now we're sitting here in a-million-dollar-plus facility with these trucks that are basically a multi-tool. We do flood work in this. We do fires, car accidents, house fires.

Lauren Wilson: We're coming into a family of a long line of firefighters. I believe there is that little bit of pressure. I can remember when I first told my father-in-law that I had joined, the first thing he said to me was, "As long as you can operate a pump, you'll be fine."

Coy Wire: As a volunteer service, recruits come from all walks of life and require intense training before being deployed.

Andrew Hain: It's a huge amount of effort. A lot of hours go into training a new recruit. It's not for bragging rights; it's because they've got to go out on the truck with you. You need to be able to work with everybody from different backgrounds. You know, people that work in corporate, people that work in construction, you'd name it. We've probably got it.

Part B How Climate Change Is Impacting Antarctica?

News Anchor: Our expedition to Antarctica. Amy Robach and her intrepid crew exploring the sites of getting up close and personal to the elusive wildlife. And see first-hand of rapidly changing climate. She has joined us once again live right now. Amy, good morning to you.

Amy: Good morning. Isn't it incredible that we can come live to you from Antarctica? Specifically, we are in Lindblad Bay. And this area was named after the founder of Lindblad expeditions, which is taking us on this unbelievable, otherworldly journey on this ship called *Endurance*. It's pretty remarkable that we can cut through this incredible field of ice.

Amy: And you talked about how unpredictable and extreme it is here in Antarctica. So we have to go from Plan A to Plan B to Plan C. Everyday things change so quickly. We were supposed to be on a kayak this morning. That was the plan. We were gonna be in a kayak and we were gonna be showing you some really incredible glacial icebergs. But you can see now we are surrounded by a field, a massive field of sea ice, and this sea ice is so critical to the animals who call home, Antarctica home. And we have been seeing many of those animals.

Amy: I believe we've got some images for you. Two of these majestic seals and we've seen so many of them. The ones we've been seeing mostly are crabeater seals. They're misnamed because there are no crabs here, so they can't eat crabs but they eat krill. But we have seen them on this ice. This is how they survive. This is how they fish. Many of the animals. You've seen penguins on this ice, feed off the nutrients underneath it.

Amy: And so the problem here with climate change as the temperatures rise, this ice is shrinking. We know that in Antarctica during the winter, doubles in size because of the ice, but we talked to one expert here on the ship who says the sea ice has already disappeared by 30% in his lifetime alone, and that rate of disappearance is accelerating. And that is the big concern.

Amy: It's not hard to imagine that 90% of the world's ice is right here in

Appendix I Scripts

	Antarctica, and as temperatures rise and ice starts to melt. This affects every single person on this planet. We talked to someone who told us on this ship what happens in Antarctica doesn't stay in Antarctica. And that's a really important lesson for us all as we discuss climate change, guys.
News Anchor:	Truly highlights what's at stake for all of us, but we've also been taking Amy questions from our viewers. And one question that many have been asking is, what's the local wildlife like? And what's it like to experience them in person?
Amy:	It is breathtaking. I'm in awe. Every time I look out my window, so we just showed you some of these incredible seals, but yesterday we saw killer whales and not just a few. We saw as many as 17 killer whales around our ship and they stayed with us and not only did we see the moms and dads. We saw at least two calves that were less than a year old. They were swimming along with their parents. And it was, you could hear, everyone on the boat collectively, in awe going, oh my gosh, running to either side of the boat to capture these beautiful animals. And we're told it's fairly rare to see a group, this large. I was told this tour could go on, this trip could go on 10 different times and you would only see one or sometimes none. So, we were really overwhelmed by seeing that incredible sight.
Amy:	And also, the penguins, I mean, wow, to see them, operate in the wild and to see them in their rookeries, and then to go and waddle down to sea, to go fish and to eat that krill again, and to come back. It was just something that I can't even describe to see animals in their own environment. Also, I suppose, they seem completely unfazed by us. Most likely, they haven't seen humans in about two years, because there certainly haven't been tours going on because of COVID. And they just weren't that interested in us. And that was pretty cool. They were just doing their thing, and we got to watch them.
News Anchor:	Fantastic. You didn't get to go on the kayak, but you did get to see the penguins and the beautiful orcas. Amy, thank you so much for all the reporting that you've been doing. We truly appreciate it. All the images as well. Of course, stay tuned all month long as our series *Climate Crisis: Saving Tomorrow* takes an in depth look at the causes and dangers of climate change and the necessary steps to avoid further consequences.

Part C Protecting a Forest by Cutting down Christmas Trees

News Anchor: A historic ranch in Colorado was providing a bounty of good this holiday season, not just for people looking for Christmas tree, but for people who would like to cut down on homelessness. Barry Peterson explains.

Barry Peterson: At the Aspen Canyon Ranch, this is one way to thin out the forest. People braving Rocky Mountain chill and choosing a favorite Christmas tree. The only charge, a donation to the Denver-based Dolores Project, which gives shelter to women experiencing homelessness. Margie and Don Mosley hunted deep into the thick underbrush.

Man 1: Yeah? Ready for me to cut it?

Woman: Yeah. Look at it from all sides. Yeah, that looks perfect.

Man 2: Perfect with a purpose. Everybody who's taking home a Christmas tree is in fact contributing to make this a healthier place.

Man 3: Right, so they'll cut a Christmas tree in an area that we haven't treated yet.

Barry Peterson: After being a dude ranch, then a marijuana B&B came bankruptcy. Phillip Xavier took over and is working with the Colorado State Forest Service on a three-year plan. Going from this to this, spacing the trees, and clearing the underbrush to prevent this.

Man 3: If there were 100 trees, there might be 15 left, and they now have space between them. They can grow. They can get water. And so the idea is, instead of having a forest fire, you create this environment where there's room between the trees. And it turns into a healthy forest again.

Barry Peterson: When he is done, he will sell the ranch to Project Sanctuary, a group that brings military families together in a wilderness setting to reconnect after long deployments.

Man 3: There's going to be hundreds of people affected positively because of this experience. The family fishing on the river, hanging out, hiking. We have beautiful lakes.

Man 2: And it will help heal.

Man 3: It will. There'll be hundreds if not thousands of people affected by this opportunity to come out here and hang out.

Barry Peterson: Meanwhile, the Mosley's tree has gone from its forest home to their home, where grandson three-year-old Monty is a forest firefighting tree trimmer in the making.

Man 4: What do you want for Christmas?

Boy: A chainsaw.

Man 4: What do you do with the chainsaw, man?

Boy: Cut down trees.

Barry Peterson: And with more trees cut down, the better chance the rest will survive and just maybe become next year's point of Christmas joy. Barry Peterson, CBS News in the Rocky Mountains.

Part D How China's New National Parks Are Protecting Biodiversity?

Reporter: I'm a conservation photographer and writer and I spent the last seven years traveling through China's most wild and stunning landscapes.

Reporter: 现在我们要准备进竹林。(Now we are going to enter the bamboo forest)

Reporter: 我们到了×××上面特别大的冰川。(Can you imagine the huge glacier above?)

Reporter: Beautiful sunset!

Reporter: Along the way I have been fortunate to travel and work with experts and rangers across China, people who are devoting their lives to one goal: the preservation of its beautiful natural habitats and diverse wildlife. Most know that China is the world's most populated country, but what really sets China apart is the diversity of its flora, fauna, and wildlife? It has the third highest species count in the world, far more than any country its size. What is also interesting is the approach to conservation. Rather than creating some national parks based on beauty, China's approach to conserving its wildlife is a bit different. This year, they are finishing 10 inaugural national parks which prioritize and focus on preserving biodiversity.

Rose Niu: 中国是一个国土面积非常大的国家，而且地貌非常多样。从海南的这热带雨林一直到这个喜马拉雅山上面的这种极寒的天气。那么由于这种多样性，地形地貌和气候类型的多样性，导致中国的生物多样性是非常丰富的。中国有34 000种的植物和动物物种。所以说呢，中国在生物多样性保护和这个荒野地保护方面的这个成就对全球的生物多样性保护的未来是非常重要的。(China is a very large country and the landforms are very diverse, from the tropical rainforest in Hainan to the extreme cold weather in the Himalayas. Because of this diverse topography, landforms, and climate types, China's biodiversity is very rich. There are 34,000 species of plants and animals in China. Therefore, China's achievements in biodiversity conservation and wilderness protection are very important to the future of global biodiversity conservation.)

Reporter: China's national parks are totally redefining how wildlife and nature will be protected and experienced in China. The first national park and the largest is Sanjiangyuan where my friend Liu Yuhan is an expert.

Reporter: Hi, 刘雨涵，好久不见。(Long time no see, Liu Yuhan.)

Yuhan Liu: 好久不见。(Long time no see.)

Reporter: 你最近怎么样？(How are you doing?)

Yuhan Liu: 最近还不错。(Good.)

Reporter: 我知道你之前在三江源国家公园待了一年的时间做研究。(I know you spent a year in Sanjiangyuan National Park doing research.) Uh, so can you tell us how were the local Tibetans involved as rangers in Sanjiangyuan? What were they protecting in the Sanjiangyuan National Park?

Yuhan Liu: 三江源其实是世界上生物多样性最为丰富的一个地区。那这个地区有很多大型的食肉动物，比如说像雪豹、金钱豹、狼、猞猁等。这些呢其实都是牧民检测员监护监测和保护的目标。他们会进行反盗猎巡护，也会和科研人员一起去放置红外相机来监测野生动物。与此同时，很多人也会帮忙去清理河道，还有山上的垃圾，让整个环境变得更加整洁一些。(Sanjiangyuan is actually one of the most biologically diverse areas in the world. There are many large carnivores in this area, for example, snow leopard, leopard, wolf, lynx, etc. These are the targets of monitoring and protection by forest monitors. They will conduct anti-poaching patrols as well as placing infrared cameras with scientific researchers to monitor wildlife. At the same time, people help to clean up the garbage in the riverway and the mountains so that the environment becomes cleaner.)

Reporter: The incredible beauty and fascination of exploring China's biodiversity with the people who work to protect it is what has kept me here for so long. In October 2021, China hosted its first COP15 session in Kunming. The country is looking to take a greater leadership role in the world for biodiversity and wilderness protection. More countries will urbanize as they progress economically there will be many challenges in the years ahead. But a global push to conserve the richness and diversity of our world that is participated in and in part led by China is something to look forward to. I look forward to following the progress and in the meantime I'll keep exploring.

Appendix II Key to Exercises

Unit 1 Education

Part A

Exercise 1 B

Exercise 2

1. unknowns   2. generated   3. plethora   4. catch   5. master
6. collegiate   7. accessible   8. viable   9. authenticity   10. capsule

Part B

1. D   2. B   3. B   4. A   5. A

Part C

1. F   2. T   3. T   4. F   5. F

Unit 2 People

Part A

Exercise 1 C

Exercise 2

1. hidden dream   2. resonates   3. spectacle   4. mobilized   5. drawn
6. at stake   7. sweeping   8. slave owners   9. reference   10. crippled

Part B

1. D   2. C   3. B   4. B   5. D

Part C

1. F 2. T 3. T 4. T 5. T

Unit 3   Food

Part A

Exercise 1 C

Exercise 2

1. DNA   2. specialty   3. crunchy   4. closed-oven   5. Intangible
6. radiating   7. differently   8. fruit trees   9. secured   10. craving

Part B

1. D 2. B 3. A 4. C 5. D

Part C

1. T 2. F 3. T 4. F 5. T

Unit 4   Travel

Part A

Exercise 1 B

Exercise 2

1. soaring   2. magnified   3. magnet   4. steep   5. neighboring
6. out of kilter   7. speculative   8. high season   9. ultimately   10. sustained

Part B

1. C 2. C 3. D 4. C 5. C

Part C

1. T 2. F 3. T 4. F 5. F

Appendix II Key to Exercises

Unit 5 Fashion

Part A

Exercise 1 A

Exercise 2

1. style assistant   2. review   3. shape   4. take into account   5. communication
6. emergence   7. digital   8. immersive   9. physics   10. fabric

Part B

1. B   2. A   3. B   4. B   5. A

Part C

1. F   2. T   3. T   4. T   5. F

Unit 6 Lifestyle

Part A

Exercise 1 C

Exercise 2

1. nap   2. nature effect   3. refresh   4. posts   5. a focus area
6. softer and greener   7. comfortable   8. civilian   9. park   10. take a break

Part B

1. C   2. B   3. C   4. C   5. B

Part C

1. T   2. T   3. F   4. T   5. T

Unit 7 Sports

Part A

Exercise 1 B

Exercise 2

1. gorgeous 2. moving it out 3. motivation 4. trump 5. turns out
6. concentrate 7. caveats 8. pounding 9. immersing 10. strenuous

Part B

1. C 2. D 3. B 4. C 5. D

Part C

1. F 2. F 3. T 4. T 5. F

Unit 8 Entertainment

Part A

Exercise 1 C

Exercise 2

1. consciousness 2. executive producer 3. acquired 4. late to 5. wrong spot
6. satisfaction 7. foolproof 8. yield 9. eliminating 10. phenomenon

Part B

1. A 2. B 3. B 4. C 5. C

Part C

1. F 2. T 3. T 4. F 5. T

Unit 9 Business

Part A

Exercise 1 C

Exercise 2

1. $175 billion 2. at a loss 3. collapsed 4. depositors 5. bank run
6. stability 7. ease those fears 8. bank there 9. confident 10. capitalism

Part B

1. C 2. A 3. C 4. B 5. D

Part C

1. T 2. F 3. T 4. F 5. F

Unit 10 Technology

Part A

Exercise 1 B

Exercise 2

1. crashed   2. fined   3. wild west   4. representing   5. shuttle
6. declined   7. equal   8. track   9. guinea pigs   10. accountability

Part B

1. A 2. D 3. D 4. C 5. B

Part C

1. F 2. F 3. T 4. T 5. F

Unit 11 Literature

Part A

Exercise 1 B

Exercise 2

1. critics   2. thriller   3. superstar   4. series   5. psychological
6. phenomenally   7. contemporary   8. afford   9. guarantee   10. heralded

Part B

1. C 2. D 3. B 4. A 5. C

Part C

1. F 2. F 3. T 4. T 5. F

Unit 12   Nature

Part A

Exercise 1   A

Exercise 2

1. suffered   2. habitats   3. bushfires   4. spark   5. trailers
6. multi-tool 7. father-in-law 8. recruits 9. bragging 10. construction

Part B

1. D 2. D 3. D 4. C 5. B

Part C

1. T 2. F 3. T 4. F 5. F